DEHYDRATING

FD

DEHYDRATING
FD

A Beginner's Guide

Jay Bills
&
Shirley Bills

Skyhorse Publishing

Skyhorse Publishing books may be purchased in bulk at special discounts for sales promotion, corporate gifts, fund-raising, or educational purposes. Special editions can also be created to specifications. For details, contact the Special Sales Department, Skyhorse Publishing, 307 West 36th Street, 11th Floor, New York, NY 10018 or info@skyhorsepublishing.com.

Skyhorse® and Skyhorse Publishing® are registered trademarks of Skyhorse Publishing, Inc.®, a Delaware corporation.

Visit our website at www.skyhorsepublishing.com.

10

Library of Congress Cataloging-in-Publication Data

Bills, Jay.
  Dehydrating food : a beginner's guide / Jay and Shirley Bills.
    p. cm.
  ISBN 978-1-60239-945-7 (pb : alk. paper)
  1. Food--Drying. 2. Food--Drying--Equipment and supplies. I. Bills, Shirley. II. Title.
  TX609.B52 2010
  641.4'4--dc22
                              2010012564

Printed in China

Nesco FD-39 Food Dehydrator.
© The Metal Ware Corporation.

« TABLE OF CONTENTS »

« Introduction: Ere You Begin . . . »

Welcome to the exciting world of food dehydrating! In this book, you will find the practical application of techniques applied to an ancient art of food preservation!

For centuries, man and nature have been preserving foods by reducing their water content down to about 10 percent. In this drying process, almost the full nutritional value is maintained, and, in dehydrated form, the foods may be stored in a comparatively small space for long periods of time.

Preserving foods by drying is certainly not the only available method, but in these critical times it offers a safe, practical, and delicious way of providing nutritional essentials. This method is available to all who are willing to observe a few basic guidelines.

Most of the information presented here has been developed by research in our own kitchen. We do not claim this book to be all-inclusive. We caution the readers and users of this book to be aware of the fact that best results are only achieved through accurate control of temperature and air flow. This, of course, can be achieved in several ways, but we feel that a well-designed commercial dehydrator will produce the best results, and if used according to our recommendations, produces a delicious product, as many users have discovered.

We are on constant alert to improve our product and our book and realize that many friends will develop interesting and practical improvements by their own experimentation. We invite and solicit your ideas and comments.

Appreciation is expressed to the following for their help, suggestions, and encouragement in our endeavors: D.K. Salunkhe, PhD, Professor of Plant Science, Utah State University; Flora H. Bardwell, Extension Foods and Nutrition Specialist, Utah State University; Glen W. Hancey; Dorothy P. Bills; R. N. Malouf, MD; and Edward and Leah Kearney—all good and well-qualified friends who live here with us in Cache Valley, Utah. We have also quoted with permission from *Canning and Other Methods of Food Preservation*, published by the Home Service Department of Duquesne Light Company, Pittsburgh, Pennsylvania (out of print).

It is our hope that this book will be a motivating guide to help people enjoy and utilize the full potential of the foods that are available. May you all have happy and delicious experiences!

Sincerely,
Jay and Shirley Bills
The Authors

CHAPTER I

« GENERAL OBSERVATIONS
ON FOOD DEHYDRATING »

WHY FOOD STORAGE?

It's smart to store food! The importance of a careful family program for storing food has been recognized for centuries. Until the invention of modern appliances and conveniences, proper food storage was essential for survival. With the development of modern

American Harvest/Nesco FD-1020 Gardenmaster Food Dehydrator.
© Pleasant Hill Grain.

technology and transportation, many people have come to feel that the need for food storage no longer exists. There is value in food preservation, however, and a food storage program will benefit the average family in many ways:

1. Planning ahead to preserve seasonal foods means it can be enjoyed all year.
2. In times of crises, adequate food storage provides a life-saving source of nutrition and gives a very fine sense of security.
3. A food storage program provides a method to help reduce the cost of food. If food is purchased when it is most abundant, the price is lower.
4. Dried food can provide delicious supplements to available—though oft-times limited—fresh foods.
5. Surplus food can be dehydrated to avoid food waste. For instance, fruit that is too ripe for canning or dehydrating can be used in fruit leather. Every part can be used—celery tops may be dehydrated, for instance, and used in soups or casserole recipes.

TYPES OF FOOD STORAGE

There are a number of types of food storage available to the average family. Each has a place and should be utilized in providing for family nutritional needs. The following are methods that can be used:

1. Dehydrating or Drying
2. Canning
3. Freezing
4. Salting or Brining
5. Root Cellars
6. Jams and Jellies
7. Smoking
8. Sprouting of Stored Seeds

Nesco fd-1010 Gardenmaster Food Dehydrator.
©The Metal Ware Corporation.

If a family uses all of the above methods, they will have a varied and well-balanced diet from their own cupboard.

The scope of this book, however, will be limited to the discussion of the most widely-used method throughout the world: dehydrating (or drying) fruits, vegetables, herbs, and meats.

DEHYDRATING: AN ANCIENT PROCESS

"Drying is a method of preserving food products in which so much of the product's natural moisture is removed that spoilage micro-organisms (yeasts, molds, and bacteria), even though present in a living condition, are unable to grow or multiply.

"The process is not new, but the method is; the process is as old as the bees. The bees collect nectar from flowers and store it in small cells where the drones, or the workers, keep up a flow of warm air over them. The warm air takes away the moisture leaving concentrated honey.

"Since the beginning of time, man has cured (dried) hay and grass, corn, herbs, and meat for animal and human consumption by the heat of the sun. In food preservation today, we accomplish this curing or drying by evaporating the moisture or water in food products from a liquid to a vapor. Heat and air are required to accomplish this, but the heat must be held at a temperature that will not affect the texture, color, flavor, or nutritional value of the product.

"Heat evaporates the water from the product, and air circulating around it absorbs the vapor. Drying changes the appearance of products, but if properly dried and stored, very few of the original food nutrients are lost.

Timucua Indians smoking game in Florida circa 1562. Drawings by Jacques le Moyne.

"Drying has the great advantage of minimizing storage problems. The dried product's weight is from one-fourth to one-tenth, or in some cases even less, compared to the fresh product. Then, too, it can be kept almost indefinitely, if stored under the proper condition."[1]

DEHYDRATING RETAINS NUTRITIONAL VALUES

Fresh fruits and vegetables are the richest sources of vitamins, minerals, sugars, proteins, and other nutritive substances essential to good health. How necessary it is then, that we do our utmost to conserve these nutrients. Even though harvested or gathered, fruits and vegetables remain living materials capable of carrying on their own life's processes. After the product is removed from its life source, these processes, if left unchecked, destroy quality because they include the oxidation of valuable materials within the product.

"The chemical changes that impair product quality, as well as attacks by organisms of decay, can be retarded by storing products in the refrigerator until processed, but this storage must be as short a time as possible; two days should be the maximum length of time.

"Only products in prime condition should be dried, and that means they are at their best for drying when they have reached maturity and are garden or orchard fresh."[2]

---

[1]Duguesne Light Company, *Canning and Other Methods of Food Preservation* (Pittsburgh, Pennsylvania: 1943 [Out of print]), pg. 71.
[2]*Ibid.*, pg. 72.

Dehydrated fruits and vegetables which have been reconstituted and cooked provide approximately the same amount of carbohydrates, fats, proteins, minerals, and bulk as the original fresh material similarly prepared. The proteins and minerals in dehydrated foods after reconstituting are no different from those of the original foods if dehydrated at the recommended proper temperature. Since steaming vegetables helps to retain more of the nutrients than scalding does, we recommend following the directions in the section on dehydrating vegetables.

"Fruits and vegetables not only provide important dietary nutrients, but make other contributions to the normal functioning of the body. Fruits, with exception of cranberries, plums, and prunes; vegetables, with the exception of rhubarb, spinach, and chard, exert an alkaline effect when oxidized in the body. The free acids and acid salts of fruits and vegetables are oxidized to carbonic acid which is eliminated by breathing. Vegetables provide salts of the metals calcium, magnesium, potassium and sodium, which are available for the purpose of neutralizing acid by products resulting from the metabolism of meat, egg, milk, and cereal proteins. This is but one of several reasons why a diet should include fruits and vegetables."[3]

Fruits are an excellent source of Vitamins A and C but are not very rich in Vitamin B-1 (Thiamin). While sulfuring destroys Vitamin B-1 in fruits, it tends to retain the potency of Vitamins A and C. It is always better to preserve the greater amount of vitamins.

"Thiamin is well retained in vegetables that have been steamed, and steaming will aid in preserving some of the Vitamin C of vegetables, which, unfortunately, is easily destroyed. Vitamin B-2 (Riboflavin) occurring in a few fruits and many vegetables, is resistant to oxidation, heat, and sulfur fumes, but is affected by light. . . . Niacin. . . . occurs

---

[3]*Ibid.*, pg. 72.

in few vegetables. It is not destroyed by oxidation or by heating to the temperature of boiling, so there should be little loss of Niacin in the process of dehydration."[4]

It is clear that dehydrated fruits and vegetables retain almost all the nutritional values possessed by the foods when they are fresh.

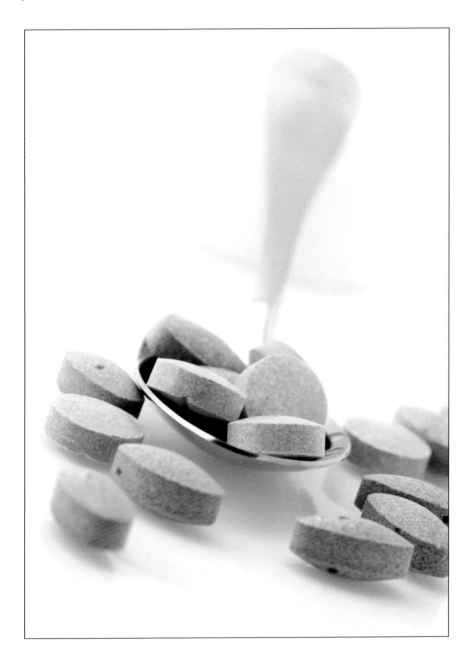

[4]*Ibid.*, pg. 85.

Nesco FD-39 Food Dehydrator.
© The Metal Ware Corporation.

METABOLIC CONSIDERATIONS RELATED TO DEHYDRATED FOODS

(The material in this section has been prepared by Dr. R.N. Malouf, MD)

Dehydrated foods are now of special interest to the general public and may have significant clinical application to those who have blood sugar symptoms. Medical sciences have established the fact that all cells in the body require a proper balance of oxygen and various nutrients in order to facilitate the vital process of physiological combustion which in turn provides needed energy and metabolic essentials which are necessary to maintain good health.

The gasoline engine is a dramatic example of the principle in point: It is a well-known fact that too much fuel causes the engine to "choke" and too little will cause the engine to "starve." The blood sugar in the body is comparable to the gasoline for the engine and is the digested simplified sugar which is directly available to the cells for combustion. If the blood sugar level is too high, then proper combustion does not take place and a *hyperglycemic* or diabetic condition may prevail. If too low, a *hypoglycemic* condition or so-called "low blood sugar" may occur and cause undesirable clinical symptoms. Therefore, it is vital to good health that there be a proper ratio between oxygen and the available blood sugar in order to provide the ideal circumstances for the all-important physiological combustion.

When natural foods are eaten and subjected to the normal digestive processes, the blood sugar rises gradually, maintains a longer effective peak level, and then gradually declines to a level which signals the need for additional nourishment. In contrast to this, the more highly concentrated sweeter foods tend to send the blood sugar up much faster, the peak level time is shorter, and the let-down is usually much quicker and may be followed by undesirable clinical symptoms.

The type of diet that people eat plays a very important role in proper body metabolism. Ideally, the more natural foods provide the best sources for energy and tissue-building nutrients. Super-sweet and highly concentrated foods oftentimes cause undesirable physiological problems. Dehydrated foods provide an excellent source of natural nutrition and should be considered in any realistic dietary regime.

When prepared in the right manner, these foods are highly palatable, very flavorful, and provide excellent nutritional values without the undue stress of overeating. It has been noted by many people that eating very small servings of dehydrated foods satisfies the feeling of hunger and yields high energy returns. Another attractive feature is the fact that when prepared as directed, these foods can be stored in a comparatively small space at room temperature thereby offering a definite storage advantage.

In conclusion, it can be empirically stated that the intake, digestion, metabolism, and subsequent physiological functions of the body are much better with more natural foods. Thus, dehydrated foods offer some very definite and desirable advantages and may well take a distinct place in the medical world of good nutrition.

CHAPTER II

« Methods of Dehydrating »

A number of different methods have been used to dehydrate fruits and vegetables. Each has its advantages and disadvantages, and you should carefully study each to decide which method will best suit the needs of your family. The needs of a family who will dehydrate a few items in small quantities during the year are obviously different from that of a large family who will dehydrate bushels of a number of different kinds of fruits, vegetables, and meats.

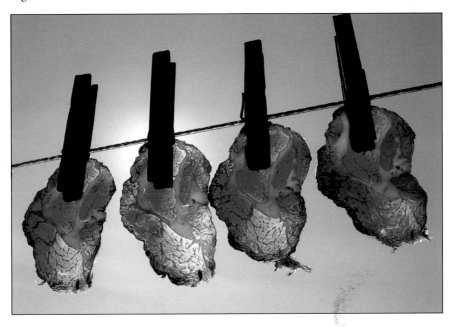

Slices of meat being sun dried.

Method 1: Sun Drying

"This method is perhaps the oldest known method of food preservation. It is the evaporation of water from products by solar or sun heat, assisted by movements of surrounding air. Products are spread on containers of one kind or another (such as window screen) that are tilted toward the south to receive the full effect of direct sunlight.

An example of tomatoes being sun dried.

"Sun drying is not the most satisfactory method. To be successful, it demands a rainless season of bright sunshine and high temperature, coinciding with a period of vegetable and fruit maturity. Sun drying requires considerable care. The products must be protected from insects with screen or netting, and must be carried into a shelter when the dust blows or rain falls and before the dew falls in the evening. If there is not a succession of sunny days, there is danger of spoilage. This method is slow at best because the sun does not cause rapid evaporation of moisture.

"Before storing, sun-dried products should be placed in an artificial heat dryer for 20–30 minutes. This will complete the drying and destroy any bacteria that may have collected during the drying process."[1]

Artificial heat in drying, such as is found in a well-designed dehydrator, has many advantages over sun drying: it can be used independently of weather conditions, it is ready to operate whenever the product is mature, it can be controlled, it can be continuous, it is a faster process, the products better retain their natural color, and flavor and nutrients are preserved to a much greater degree.

METHOD 2: USE OF A NET BAG

Food can be prepared and placed in a net bag and hung on the clothesline. Again, the advantage of this method is that it requires very little investment and keeps the insects and birds out. However, the bag must be brought in each night and any time it rains, and the bag should be shaken regularly to redistribute food so it will dry thoroughly and evenly. It will work—but is an obviously limited method and leaves much to be desired.

METHOD 3: OVEN DRYING

Fruits and vegetables can be dried in the oven. The kitchen should be well ventilated and care must be taken to keep the heat low. Set the regulator at 140–145°F and preheat the oven. When the product is first placed in the oven, the temperature will drop, but it will soon build up. Do not let the temperature rise above 145°F.

When drying either fruits or vegetables in an electric oven, leave the door open two inches. When using a gas oven, the door must be open eight inches. This helps to control temperature, but is also necessary to allow the escape of moisture through air circulation.

"If an oven with a regulator is not available, a portable oven thermometer is a great convenience although you can learn to tell by the 'feel' of the product whether or not it is drying satisfactorily. It should feel moist and slightly cooler than the air flowing over it. If it does not, it is drying too fast."[2]

The food may be placed in pans or trays; trays made of open mesh material speed the drying process. Tray frames may be made of inch or inch-and-a-half lumber.

---

[1] *Ibid.*, pg. 73.
[2] *Ibid.*, pg. 73.

The frames should be small enough to fit on the oven racks. Cover the frames with any open mesh material, such as curtain netting, cheese cloth, muslin, or strong, washable nylon netting. If necessary, reinforce the covering by stretching strings diagonally across the frame underneath. This will keep the cloth from sagging. Spread the prepared product on the trays one layer deep and place the trays on the oven racks. Stir the product and rotate the trays occasionally to insure even drying.

The disadvantages of oven drying are many: It is difficult to get sufficient air movement, it can be difficult to get a low enough temperature in your oven to preserve nutrients and color, two racks are not efficient when dehydrating large amounts, and the oven is now not available for any other use.

Method 4: Dehydrators

Home-Built:

Constructing a home-built dehydrator that will produce the highest quality end-product is a very difficult task for the home handyman to attempt.

1. *Wooden Frame Box*
   A dehydrator can be constructed from a wooden box into which an electric heating element or a gas burner and a fan have been installed. This gives better control over

L'Equip Filter Pro Food Dehydrator.
© Pleasant Hill Grain.

temperature and air movement, but it becomes difficult to clean and may absorb food odors. Considerable experimentation is required to get the right air movement and temperature in home-built units in order to achieve optimum drying conditions.

2. *Refrigerator*

An old refrigerator can be used to make a dehydrator by adding a fan, shelf supports, and a heating element. This provides more control and is easier to clean, but it does require some skill with sheet metal work and takes experimenting to get the right

Nesco 1020 Food Dehydrator.
© *The Metal Ware Corporation.*

temperature and air movement. It is also very bulky for the space used and is difficult to store or move.

COMMERCIALLY-BUILT UNITS:

1. *Speed*: "Whatever the method of drying, by sunshine or by controlled heat, speed is the word to keep in mind, both when preparing fresh foods for the drying and when starting the drying process. The faster you work the higher will be the vitamin value of the dried food, and the better the color, flavor, and cooking quality."[3]

2. *Temperature*: Authorities recommend a maintained temperature of 140–145°F in cabinet-type dryers. If the temperature is too low, food may sour and spoil.

    Dr. D.K. Salunkhe of Utah State University states that food dehydrated at 160°F will lose three times as many vitamins as food dehydrated at 140–145°F.

    Surface drying and souring is prevented by controlling temperature and air flow. The proper temperature is, of course, obtained by increasing or decreasing the heat source. When controlled by a thermostatically-operated heat source, the temperature should remain fairly constant in the loaded operating cabinet. When products first start to dry, there is little danger of scorching, but when nearly dry, they scorch easily (and scorching destroys flavor as well as nutritive value).

3. *Circulation of Air*: When still air has absorbed all the moisture it can hold, then no further evaporation can take place from a moist object. Therefore, provision must be made to remove the moist air and replace it with dry air so that evaporation can continue. "If, however, the surface moisture is evaporated more quickly than the inner tissues are diffusing it to the surface, then the surface hardens, the inner moisture cannot get through and the drying is retarded. This surface drying is called 'case hardening.'"[4] In the well-designed dehydrator, proper air circulation is accomplished by an air-cooled fan.

    "Drying is best accomplished when the process is a continuous one because growth of micro-organisms is held to a minimum, whereas when heat is applied intermittently, temperatures conducive to bacterial growth can develop."[5]

4. *Convenience*: The several racks provide increased drying capacity. Dehydrating can be accomplished during the night. The unit does not need to be placed in an area that needs ventilating. We have dehydrated our food in our basement, for instance, with no appreciable difference in humidity.

    Root vegetables, such as carrots, potatoes, onions, and cabbage, can be stored in a root cellar until the winter season and can then be dehydrated at your convenience. However, when vegetables such as carrots and potatoes are stored for an extended period of time, the starch in the vegetables converts to sugar, and this condition extends the dehydrating time by an appreciable amount.

---

[3]*Ibid.*, pg. 72.
[4]*Ibid.*, pg. 72.
[5]*Ibid.*

CHAPTER III
« Basic Dehydrating Techniques »

Most fruits and vegetables can be dehydrated. However, since personal tastes differ, it becomes a personal matter as to which fruits and vegetables are to be preserved. In this book, we have tried to present basic guidelines on work we have done, but do not intend to imply these are the only products that can be dehydrated.

Fruits and vegetables selected for dehydrating should be in prime condition. Fruits should be firm; if poor quality fruit is used, the dried product will also be of poor quality. The same rule applies to vegetables and herbs.

The two essentials in dehydrating fruits and vegetables are proper temperature and proper air flow; this information is fully discussed in the previous chapter.

Snackmaster FD-35 Entree-5 Tray.
© *The Metal Ware Corporation.*

17

Chart Number 1: Preparation Chart
Raw Fruits or Vegetables

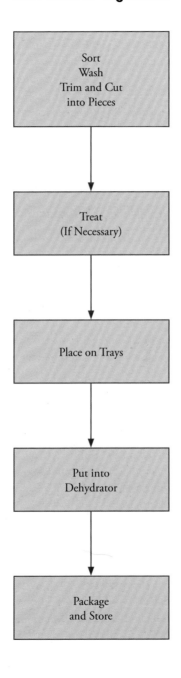

Experiments have been made with several different materials to support fruit during the dehydrating process. It has been found that high sugar-content fruits such as bananas will stick to the shelves and become very difficult to remove. This sticking tendency may be prevented by using nylon netting. The hole size of the netting should be large enough to permit adequate air flow, but small enough so that items such as peas and corn will not fall through.

However, do not wash the netting in an automatic washer: If it runs through the spin cycle, the wrinkles will be set and cannot be removed. Wash in sudsy water, rinse, and pat dry. With proper care, this heavy nylon netting can be used indefinitely.

Both fruits and vegetables must be prepared in such a way that the moisture can get out. This can be accomplished either by peeling or slicing. If the skin is left intact, the moisture cannot escape as readily and the dehydrating time will be exceptionally long. Avoid the disappointment of a friend who loaded a dehydrator with whole prunes and after three days accepted the fact they were not going to dehydrate in a reasonable length of time.

Accessory Equipment Needed for Dehydrating

Keep the equipment you use for dehydrating simple, but effective. Items you will need are:

1. Deep pan with a close-fitting lid (used for blanching)
2. Perforated rack, wire basket, or colander to fit into pan to hold products (used for blanching)
3. Stainless steel knives (carbon steel will discolor fruit)
4. Large pan to hold Erythorbic Acid or Ascorbic Acid solution
5. Kitchen timer

Nesco/American Harvest FD-39 Food Dehydrator.
© The Metal Ware Corporation.

6. Sulfur cabinet with wooden racks (if using an intermittent heat source, such as the sun)
7. Dehydrating unit (i.e., wooden box, oven, or commercially built unit)
8. Nylon netting to place on shelves
9. Container for dried products; jars or cans with tight-fitting lids or heavy plastic bags that can be heat-sealed.

CHAPTER IV
« USING PRESERVATIVES »

PRESERVATIVES

Many people do not wish to use preservatives of any kind. If you are going to dehydrate fruit for a short storage life, (i.e., six to nine months) no preservatives are needed. However, if you plan to store fruits for a longer period of time, you should use some type of preservative. This preserves color and decreases the loss of vitamins and therefore preserves the nutritional value of food.

The method of preserving vegetables through blanching is discussed in the section on dehydrating vegetables.

One method of preserving natural fruit color and flavor is to dip the fruit in one of the following solutions:

Erythorbic Acid or Ascorbic Acid: Dip fruit for two minutes only in a solution of one tablespoon Erythorbic Acid or Ascorbic Acid dissolved in one gallon of water. This preparation retards oxidation and prevents darkening of light-colored fruits during the dehydrating process.

Sodium Bisulfite Solution: Dip fruit for two minutes only in a solution of one tablespoon sodium bisulfite to one gallon water. Sodium bisulfite helps to keep fruit from darkening during the storage period. Drain thoroughly.

Combination of Sodium Bisulfite and Ascorbic or Erythorbic Acid: Another method is to use a combination of one tablespoon sodium bisulfite and one tablespoon Erythorbic Acid or Ascorbic Acid dissolved in one gallon of water. This method preserves the quality and color during the dehydrating process and during the storage period. If you plan to dry your fruit in the sun, it should definitely be sulfured because the heat source is not controlled and constant. However, if the fruit is dried in a well-designed dehydrator where this heat source is controlled and constant, less oxidation occurs and the fruit retains more of its color.

For those who are concerned with the intake of sulfur into the human body, Dr. D. K. Salunkhe at Utah State University states: "The body needs sulfur, which is part of a certain type of protein." Moderate exposure of fruits to sulfur fumes (as outlined below) is definitely beneficial to the product when using an intermittent heat source, and is not toxic to the health of the consumer. The heat of drying and subsequent cooking dissipates practically all of the sulfur.

SULFURING

Another method of preserving natural fruit color and flavor in fruit is sulfuring with a compartment. "It may be a box, provided it is large enough to cover the trays and a sulfur pan. The sulfur pan may be any shallow pan or metal lid, such as a baking powder can lid. A packing box may be covered with roofing paper or tarpaulin, or a compartment may be built out of wallboard or a cardboard box. A small opening must be provided near the bottom of the container for ventilation. Sulfur will not burn without it. All sulfuring should be performed out of doors. The opening should be closed after the sulfur has all burned so as to retain the fumes long enough to "cure" the product.

TRAY	wooden ones are needed for the product as sulfur corrodes metal.
BLOCKS	of wood or brick placed on the ground may be used to support the trays.
STACK	them one upon the other with something between each one to provide circulation. The lowest tray should be six to eight inches from the ground.
PLACE	the sulfur pan in front of the trays.
MEASURE	one level teaspoonful of sulfur for each pound of prepared fruit. (A sulfur candle is also available for this use.)
WRAP	the sulfur in paper and place it on the ground.
SPREAD	the prepared product on the trays. Spread pitted fruit pit side up.
STACK	the trays and then light the paper around the sulfur. (Do not leave the match on the sulfur pan. It may prevent sulfur from burning to completion.)
PLACE	the covering compartment over trays and sulfur pan.
KEEP	product in sulfur fumes for time designated on the following chart.
REMOVE	from sulfur compartment.
TRANSFER	product to drying racks and dehydrate."[1]

Chart Number 2
Time Requirements for Sulfuring Fruits Out of Doors[2]

Fruit	Time in Minutes
Apples	60
Apricots	60, sliced
	120, quartered
Cherries (White)	10–15
Peaches	60, sliced
	120, quartered
Pears	60, sliced
	120, quartered
Plums, large	60, sliced
	120, quartered
Prunes	60, sliced
	120, quartered
Nectarines	60, sliced
	120, quartered

---

[1] *Ibid.*, pg. 78.
[2] Flora H. Bardwell and Dr. D. K. Salunkhe, *Home Drying of Fruits and Vegetables* (Logan, Utah: Utah State University Extension).

Sliced oranges ready to be dehydrated.

Chart Number 3: Conversion Chart

Fresh, Dehydrated, and Reconstituted Relationships: Fruits

The following chart is provided as an aid in learning how to convert fresh fruit to dehydrated and to reconstitute and then use the dehydrated fruit in recipes calling for either fresh or canned fruit.

PRODUCT	THIS AMOUNT FRESH WEIGHT[1] POUNDS	YIELDS APPROXIMATELY THIS AMOUNT DEHYDRATED WEIGHT POUNDS	THIS AMOUNT DEHYDRATED CUPS	THIS AMOUNT DEHYDRATED Wt. Oz.	PLUS THIS AMOUNT WATER CUPS	YIELDS APPROXIMATELY THIS AMOUNT RECONSTITUTED CUPS	YIELDS APPROXIMATELY THIS AMOUNT RECONSTITUTED Wt.[2] Oz.	PLUS THIS MUCH LIQUID CUPS
APPLES	25	4	1	0.8	2	1¼	4.2	1½
APRICOTS	25	5	1	2.2	2	1	6.7	1⅓
BANANAS	25	5	1	2.6	2	1	7.2	1¼
CHERRIES, pie	25	5	1	3.4	2	1¼	5.8	1⅔
CHERRIES, Bing	25	5	1	3.4	2	1¼	6.2	1½
GRAPES	25	5.5	1	3.5	2	1⅓	7.5	1½
PEACHES	25	5	1	1.9	2	1¼	6.6	1¼
PEARS	25	5	1	2.4	2	1	7.8	1¼
PLUMS	25	5	1	2.5	2	⅞	6.1	1⅓
PRUNES	25	5	1	3.9	2	1¼	7.6	1⅓
RHUBARB	25		1	2	2	2	8.7	1⅛
RASBERRIES	25		1	0.9	2	⅔	2.7	1⅔
STRAWBERRIES	25		1	2.2	2	1	6.3	1⅓

[1] Ready to dehydrate (peeled, etc).
[2] Soaked for 3–3½ hours.

CHAPTER V
« Dehydrating Fruit »

Most fruits and berries may be dried satisfactorily. Select fresh, firm, ripe fruit. Discard all bruised or decayed fruits. (One piece of slightly spoiled fruit may flavor the entire lot.) Select late varieties in apples.

Thoroughly clean all products. Use stainless steel knives for cutting (carbon steel will discolor fruit). Slice everything ³⁄₁₆-inch thick; as you gain experience, you will find there are some items you may not want to slice, such as apricots, prunes, plums, cherries, etc. As apples, pears, peaches, etc., are peeled, cored or pitted, and sliced, prepare only enough fruit to fill one tray at a time. Dip in prepared solution of one tablespoon Erythorbic Acid or Ascorbic Acid dissolved in one gallon water. Soak fruit slices for two minutes only and drain thoroughly. Two minutes is entirely adequate and longer soaking will lengthen the drying time considerably.

Sliced fruit is ready to be dried.

When slices are the same thickness, the fruit will dry evenly. It is not necessary, however, to measure each slice. The slices should be placed close together, just touching, but only one layer deep so there is adequate air circulation. Immediately place the slices on nylon netting on the trays and put them into a dehydrator (or oven or out-of-doors). Remember, speed is very important in preparing fruit for drying by any method.

You may then proceed to fill the other trays in the same manner until the dehydrator is filled. (Refer to Chart 4, Condensed Directions for Dehydration of Fruits.)

When dehydrating fruits such as apricots, plums, etc., the dehydrating time can be reduced by doing the following:

1. Break or cut the fruit in half and remove the pit.
2. Take one half in both hands, placing both thumbs in the middle of the skin side.
3. Turn the half "inside out." This breaks open the fibers, as you will see when this method is used, thereby reducing the drying time. With a little practice, this method is very easy and extremely effective. (We are indebted to Dora D. Flack for this idea.)

Different varieties of fruit can be dehydrated at the same time, placing a different variety on each shelf. However, do not mix fruits and vegetables in the same dehydrator load.

SPECIAL TREATMENT OF FRUIT BEFORE DEHYDRATING

These suggestions should be used only when fruit is being prepared in a dehydrator.

APPLES

You can flavor your apple slices by:

1. Lightly sprinkling various flavors of dry Jell-O on the apple slices.
2. Dipping the apple slices in lemon juice (1 tablespoon lemon juice to ½ cup water) and arranging the slices on trays. Then sprinkle on coconut that has been ground in a blender to a fine powder.
3. Dipping slices in a solution of corn syrup or honey.
4. Mixing 2 ½ pounds sugar with 5 pounds of sliced apples and let them sit overnight. In the morning, drain, put apples onto shelves, and dehydrate. Boil drained-off liquid to kill enzymes and use resulting liquid as a topping for hotcakes, etc.
5. Using fresh pineapple, pureed. Add orange-flavored Jell-O, mix well and apply, using a small paint brush or spoon to apply it onto apple rings.
6. Crush raspberries and strain the juice, adding a bit of lemon juice, and painting onto apple slices or rings.
7. Sprinkling lightly with a mixture of cinnamon and sugar.

PEARS

1. Sprinkling on various dry Jell-O flavors.
2. Sprinkling with a mixture of cinnamon and sugar.

PRUNES OR PLUMS

1. Halve prunes and remove pits; use a little bit of lemon juice on inside of prunes just to moisten. Spread this on with a little paint brush.
2. Sprinkle with either pineapple, orange, cherry, wild cherry, or black cherry dry Jell-O.

Chart Number 4
Condensed Directions for Dehydration of Fruits

It is not advisable to depend on any definite drying time when drying fruits. There are too many variables: the size of the load, the thickness of the slices, variations in temperature, the nature of the heat source, and the relative humidity of the air entering the dryer all are contributing factors. *Refer to the timing in this table as a general guide only.*

Product	Preparation	Average Drying Time (Hours)
Apples	Select late-maturing, firm ripe fruit; handle carefully as bruised spots must be trimmed out. Wash thoroughly and pare. Cut into slices 3/16" thick. Drop into solution (see section on Preservatives) and let stand two minutes before draining thoroughly. Place on netting on shelves one layer deep and place in dehydrator.	12–15
Apricots	Select tree-ripened fruit; do not peel. Cut in halves and turn inside out or slice 3/16" thick. Drop in solution for two minutes and drain. Place treated fruit on netting on shelves, skin side down and only one layer deep, and place in dehydrator.	24–36
Bananas	Select ripe, firm fruit; trim off any bruised spots. Slice 3/16" thick and drop into solution for two minutes, drain thoroughly. Put on netting on shelves and place in dehydrator.	15–24
Berries	Use firm berries; handle carefully. Wash, sort, and drain; no other treatment necessary. Slice strawberries 3/16" thick. Spread on netting on shelves, one layer deep, and place in dehydrator.	15–24
Cherries	Select fruit that is just ripe—must be firm. Wash and remove imperfect fruit. If pits are to be removed, take off stems. When pitted, let fruit drain for an hour (but reserve all juice as it may be bottled). Spread pitted, drained fruit on netting on shelves one layer deep and place in dehydrator. If cherries are cut in half, drying time will be less.	24–36

(Continued)

Chart Number 4: (Continued)

Condensed Directions for Dehydration of Fruits

Product	Preparation	Average Drying Time (Hours)
Figs, Grapes	Wash, cut out blemishes, and cut in half. Spread fruit one layer deep, skin side down on netting on shelves and dehydrate. For best results, use Thompson Seedless grapes.	15–20
Lemon or Orange Peel	Wash orange or lemon, grate on grater with at least ¼" openings until white layer is reached, but do not grate into this layer. Place grated peel on nylon netting one layer deep and dehydrate.	12–15
Pears	Select the best-eating varieties, such as Bartlett and Kieffer. If possible, pick them before they are quite ripe; store them for a week or two but use them while they are still quite firm. Wash, pare, and core, and remove blemishes. Cut into ³⁄₁₆" slices or eighths. Drop into solution for two minutes, drain, and then place fruit on netting on trays one layer deep and place in dehydrator.	15–24
Peaches	Select fully-ripe fruit that is firm enough to stand some handling. Wash the unpeeled fruit and dip fruit in boiling water for a few seconds to loosen skins, and then plunge into cold water. Remove skins, slice fruit into ³⁄₁₆" slices and drop into solution for two minutes. Drain thoroughly and place on netting on shelves one layer deep and place in dehydrator.	15–24
Plums, Prunes	Wash, cut in half, and take out pits. Turn inside out and dip in solution for two minutes; drain thoroughly and place on netting, skin side down, one layer deep and place shelves in dehydrator.	24–36
Rhubarb	Trim off imperfect places, ends, and tops. Wash, slice cross-wise into ³⁄₁₆" slices. Place on netting on shelves one layer deep and place into dehydrator.	12–15

Note: Acid fruits should not be placed directly on metal for dehydrating; cover metal shelves with washable nylon netting and place fruit on it. This can then be put directly into the dehydrator.

BANANAS

1. Sprinkle slices with dry Jell-O, cornmeal, shredded coconut, etc.

TESTING FRUIT FOR DRYNESS

It is sometimes necessary to test whether the fruit is completely dried. The following guidelines are provided to simplify the task. (Remember to cool the piece of fruit before testing).

All the fruit except rhubarb should roll easily and spring back into shape without cracking. Learn to determine by the feel of the fruit whether or not it is sufficiently dry.

STORAGE

When the fruit is dry enough, remove trays from the dehydrator and cool the fruit thoroughly. Store immediately according to the directions in the section "Storage After Dehydrating" (pg. 63). Do not leave the fruit on the trays for any length of time or the product will start reabsorbing moisture and will have to be dehydrated again.

DIRECTIONS FOR RECONSTITUTING DEHYDRATED FRUITS

General Rule: 1 cup dehydrated fruit
2 cups warm water
Do not add sugar

Let sit for one-half hour or until fruit is plump. Cook over medium heat until fruit is tender and then add sugar to taste.

If you wish to use the fruit for pies, tarts, etc., cool liquid and add thickening.

FRUIT	TESTS FOR DRYNESS
Apples	Leathery; no moist area in center
Apricots, nectarines, peaches, large plums, and prunes	Pliable; leathery; a handful properly dried will fall apart after squeezing together (If they stick together, they are not dry enough.)
Bananas	Pliable; leathery
Berries	Hard; no visible moisture when crushed; dry enough to rattle
Cherries	Leathery but sticky
Figs	Pliable; leathery
Grapes, plums, and prunes	Pliable; leathery
Lemon or orange peel	Pliable; leathery
Pears	Springy feel
Rhubarb	Brittle (feels more like a vegetable)
Strawberries	Pliable; leathery

Note: If you are going to use the dehydrated fruit to make desserts calling for fresh fruit, use: 1 cup dehydrated fruit and 1 cup warm water.

Let sit until the liquid is absorbed and the fruit is plump. Refer to the Recipe Section for specific details according to the recipe used.

Suggested Uses for Dehydrated Fruits

(Use your own imagination for additional ideas)

Product	Dehydrate							Reconstituted		
	Snacks	Raisins	Cereal	Desserts	Gelatin	Tarts Pies	Cakes	Cookies Cupcakes	Bread	Fruit Leather
Apples	X		X	X	X	X	X	X	X	X
Apricots	X		X	X	X	X	X	X	X	X
Bananas	X		X			X	X	X	X	X
Cherries, Pie	X	X		X		X	X	X		X
Cherries, Bing	X	X	X	X		X	X	X	X	X
Grapes	X	X	X				raisins	raisins	raisins	X
Peaches	X		X	X	X	X	X	X	X	X
Pears	X		X	X		X	X			X
Peel (orange, lemon)				X	X	X	X	X	X	X
Plums	X		X	X		X	X	X	X	X
Prunes	X		X	X		X	X	X	X	X
Rhubarb				X		X	X	X		X
Raspberries			X	X	X	X	X	X		X
Strawberries	X		X	X	X	X	X	X		X

Chart Number 6

Cost-Conversion Chart: Fruit

Multiply the cost of the item per pound by the factor figure provided below. The result will be the cost of a gallon of food which you dehydrate yourself.

For example, if apricots cost $3.99 per pound, 3.99 × 11 equals a cost of $43.89 per gallon of dehydrated apricots.

ITEM	FACTOR[1,2]
APPLES	4.0
APRICOTS	11.0
BANANAS	13.0
CHERRIES, Pie	17.0
CHERRIES, Bing	17.0
PEACHES	9.5
PEARS	12.0
PLUMS	12.5
PRUNES	19.5

[1] This is only an approximate cost since there are a number of factors that can cause a small change in the figure.

[2] This figure does not include any labor or container cost.

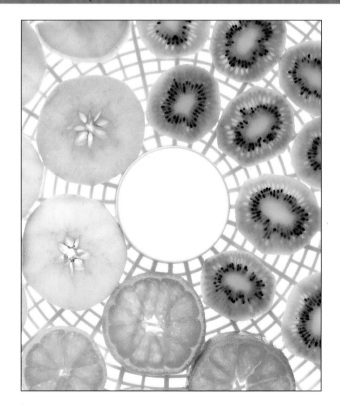

CHAPTER VI
« MAKING FRUIT LEATHER »

This section was written in conjunction with Glen W. Hancey.

DEHYDRATED FRUIT DELICACIES: FRUIT LEATHER

Fruit leather is a favorite snack food with many who have had the opportunity to try this delectable product. It is becoming more popular since commercial companies have introduced it through supermarket outlets. Children, both young and older, seem to like the natural goodness of fruit leather and will use it to satisfy their sweet tooth instead of eating candy.

Fruit leather is fruit which has been pureed into pulp, sweetened (if desired), spread on cookie sheets (or heavy aluminum foil sheets), and dehydrated. We have heard of people using all of the following equipment and methods of dehydrating (or drying) fruit leather, with varying degrees of success: commercial dehydrator, oven drying, fan drying in a warm room, and sun drying—either putting the pan on a table out in the hot sun or putting the pan in the back of a car parked in the hot sun. (If you choose to try this method, make sure you roll up the windows!)

When using a dehydrator or oven, the temperature setting should be as close to 140° as is possible. An electric oven should have the door ajar two inches; gas ovens should have the door ajar eight inches—this is to provide a means for the moist air to escape. Drying time will usually take 8–30 hours, depending on the dehydrating method used and the moisture content of the puree.

EQUIPMENT NEEDED

Blender:	preferable, but a colander, food mill, sieve, egg beater, or even a fork can be used.
Cookie sheets:	one pan, 14 × 16-inch, will hold 2 ½–3 cups puree. Heavy aluminum foil can be used by turning up edges ¾ inch to form sides. If using a dehydrator or an oven to dehydrate, use a cookie sheet that will allow air to circulate all around it. Cake pans should not be used because the sides are too high for air to circulate freely over the leather.
Plastic wrap:	Handi-Wrap or Saran Wrap is excellent; spread the wrap on the cookie sheet or on the foil sheet. This is used to prevent the puree from sticking.

Screen:	or nylon net or cheesecloth to cover the leather and to protect
(if sun-drying)	it from insects. Use spring clothespins to anchor the net to the
	edges of the cookie sheet.

BASIC DIRECTIONS

Most fruits can be made into fruit leather using the following directions: Use flavorful, ripe fruit, wash clean and remove spots, defects, etc. Fruit that is over-ripe but not spoiled can be made into a puree; old bottled or canned fruit may also be used after draining off the liquid. Most fruits can be blended with the peelings on, although there are a few exceptions to this. Pears should be peeled to eliminate the "sandy" texture found in the peel.

Peaches produce a more pleasing leather if peeled, although some prefer the peelings blended in.

When using cantaloupes, fresh pineapple, or bananas, the peel must be taken off. Remove pits from pitted fruit; section larger fruits for use in the blender. Drop fruit into the blender, one halve or piece at a time; working with more than one cup of fruit at a time is hard on the blender.

If you are rushed for time or space to dehydrate the leather, the fruit may be pureed, measured, and stored in containers in the freezer. When time and space permit, remove one package at a time, or the amount you can dehydrate at one time, allow to thaw, flavor, and proceed according to instructions.

Many fruits will not require an additional sweetener. However, if the puree is too sour or tart, add corn syrup or honey until it is as sweet as you desire. Start with ½ tablespoon of a sweetener and blend well. Honey can be heated to make it run more freely. Corn syrup or honey keeps the leather from becoming too dry and leaves it slightly tacky and a bit on the leathery side. Each person enjoys a different taste and what might be too sweet for one might be just right for another. Use your own judgment.

Any leftover fruit from regular dehydrating can be put into the puree.

Spread the puree ¼" to 5⁄16" thick evenly over the plastic wrap which has been put on the cookie sheet. If the plastic wrap is too wide and extends up the sides of the cookie sheet, cut it to fit the cookie sheet or anchor it with clothespins so it will not flop down over the edges of the leather. Do not spread the puree completely to the edges; leave a bit of plastic showing for easy removal and so the puree will not run back under the edge and onto the pan. If you are drying out-of-doors, spread screen or nylon netting or cheesecloth over the pan, anchoring it with clothespins, to keep out insects.

Dry the leather until it feels dry but still slightly tacky. The heavier the consistency of the puree and the thinner the puree is spread on the pan, the less drying time will be required. However, if the puree is spread too thin on the pan, the resulting product will be too hard and the "leather" effect will not be obtained. These "chips" resulting from leather spread too thin are still excellent to eat. When using a dehydrator, three cookie sheets can be used at a time in one load.

When the puree is dry but tacky on one side, spread another piece of plastic wrap over the top of the leather and turn the entire leather over; peel off the first piece of plastic and put the pan back to complete the drying process. The leather should be approximately ⅛" thick after dehydrating, although the finished thickness will depend on how thick the puree is spread on the pan.

When completely dry and cool, roll the leather to loosen it from the plastic wrap, then replace the plastic. Roll the plastic and leather together into a roll. Leaving the plastic wrap on will keep the leather from sticking to itself. Label each roll as you complete it, either with masking tape or label stickers. You may have to cut the roll to fit into your storage container. Store in an air-tight container, either glass jars or plastic containers with tight lids. Put in a dark, cool place (60°F or below if possible).

RECIPES FOR FRUIT LEATHER

Plain puree can be made from most fruits, such as apples, apricots, bananas, red or Bing cherries, peaches, pears, pineapple, plums, etc. However, some fruits do not make good fruit leather unless blended with another fruit. An example of this is rhubarb, which is too tart; add sweet fruits to complement it. Cantaloupe alone is not good, but blends well with other fruits when used sparingly. Extreme sours or bitters complement the sweet fruits, but are not good alone.

After enough puree has been blended to make 2 ½ cups, sweeten to taste. You may want to add spices, such as cinnamon, nutmeg, etc. The spices can either be blended into the puree—approximately ¼ teaspoon per 2 ½ cups puree—or the spice may be sprinkled on top of the puree just before dehydrating. Sprinkle coconut on top, or nuts, or use your imagination and whatever your family especially likes. Lemon juice may be added to light fruit to keep the leather from darkening; it may also be added to fruit that is extra sweet; usually 1 teaspoon to 2 cups puree.

After you have made plain fruit leather, try these combinations:

Apple-Chokecherry
> 6 cups sweet apples, not peeled
> ½ cups chokecherry juice
> 5 tablespoons honey
Variations: ½ cup finely blended coconut added to puree
> 1 cup nectarines added to puree

Apricot-Orange Peel
> 6 cups apricots (pitted and halved)
> 1 tablespoon orange bits (or dried orange peel blended fine)
> 3 ½ tablespoons honey or 6 tablespoons white corn syrup
> 1 teaspoon lemon juice
Variations: Use pineapple bits in place of orange bits—or use both

Banana-Pineapple with Orange Peel
> 2 cups peeled bananas
> 1 cup fresh pineapple (or drained, canned pineapple)
> 1 tablespoon dried, finely blended orange or tangerine peel
> 2 teaspoons lemon juice

Peach-Blue Plum
> 2 cups fresh blue plums (pitted)
> 3 cups fresh peaches (peeled and halved)
> 3 tablespoons honey with 1 tablespoon water
> 1 teaspoon lemon juice

Peach-Pear
> 2 cups peaches, washed, peeled, pitted, and halved
> 2 cups pears, washed, peeled, halved, and cored
> No sweetener necessary unless desired

½ teaspoon lemon juice
Variations: Add ½ cup cantaloupe

Strawberry-Rhubarb-Pineapple
    2 cups fresh-washed strawberries
    1 cup fresh rhubarb, washed and cut into inch pieces
    ½ cup fresh or unsweetened canned (drained) pineapple
    2 tablespoons honey
    Dash of lemon, if desired

Strawberry-Strained-Raspberry
    2 cups strawberries, washed
    2 cups raspberries, washed (blend separately and strain out seeds)
    ½ teaspoon lemon juice
    1 tablespoon honey
Variations: shredded coconut sprinkled on top of puree
        ½ cup chokecherry juice with extra tablespoon honey blended in
        Blend in 3 cups summer apples with 2 extra tablespoons honey

Seedless Grape with Apples and Boysenberry
    4 cups Thompson seedless grapes
    2 cups summer apples
    1 cup Boysenberries (strained)
    ½ teaspoon lemon juice
    2 tablespoons honey
Variations: shredded coconut lightly sprinkled on puree

Watermelon-Apple
   2 cups summer apples, cored
   2 cups watermelon (take out seeds)

Wild Huckleberry-Strained-Raspberries
   2 cups wild huckleberries
   3 cups strained raspberry puree
   1 tablespoon honey
   ½ teaspoon lemon juice
Variations: blend in 1 cup wild black currants
            blend in ½ cup wild Potawatomi Plums

Apple-Tang
   Mix 1 tablespoon Tang (orange, grape, or lemon) with apple puree before drying.
   Now try your own combinations.
   For additional information on fruit leather and recipes, refer to *Fun With Fruit Preservation*, by Dora D. Flack, (Bountiful, Utah, Horizon Publishers, 1973).

CHAPTER VII

« DEHYDRATING VEGETABLES »

SELECTING VEGETABLES FOR DEHYDRATING

"Only fresh vegetables in prime condition can produce quality in the dried product. Wilted ones should not be used; deterioration has already begun in them. One moldy bean may give a bad flavor to an entire lot.

"If possible, gather the vegetables early in the morning; prepare them and start the drying process as soon after gathering as possible."[1]

If you own a dehydrator, either one you have made or a commercially built unit, the vegetables can be dried during the night and taken out in the morning when more vegetables can then be processed. This is one more advantage to using a dehydrator.

"If you are drying by another method, vegetables gathered in the evening should be carefully sorted and cleaned and stored in the refrigerator. In the morning, prepare and dry.

---

[1] *Canning and Other Methods of Food Preservation, op. cit.*, pg. 76.

"When immature string beans (either green or yellow) and young green peas are dried, the results may be very satisfactory in appearance, flavor, and palatability. But all too frequently they undergo an enzymatic change losing flavor and developing an unpleasant hay-like odor. These vegetables, when dried, absorb moisture very quickly and this hastens the change; but, it can occur when the product is stored in hermetically sealed containers. Use full-grown, fresh, tender string beans; use peas that are full grown but gather them before the pods have turned yellow."[2]

Vegetables should be washed thoroughly, tops and roots removed, then sliced approximately 3⁄16" thick. They should be uniform in thickness so the dehydrating will be even.

THE BLANCHING PROCESS

Most vegetables, with the exception of onions, garlic, and tomatoes, must be blanched before drying either by steaming or scalding them.

Blanching reduces the number of spoilage micro-organisms in the product, stops destructive chemical changes, preserves or sets the color, checks ripening processes by stopping the enzyme action, and coagulates some of the soluble constituents, thereby saving the vitamin content. It relaxes the walls of the tissues so the moisture can escape

Steaming your food first helps to preserve the nutrients.

[2] Ibid.

readily. It also helps retard undesirable changes in flavor during storage and assures satisfactory reconstitution of the product.

The steam method is preferred because it does not leech out the nutrients during the blanching process. This is the procedure to follow:

1. Select a pan with a close-fitting lid.
2. Either purchase or make a rack for holding the vegetables above the boiling water. (We found an adjustable steamer in a local hardware store that does an excellent job.) Water should not touch the product. Put about ½" water in the pan; water should be boiling briskly before putting prepared vegetables into the pan.
3. When the vegetables are put in, slices should be separated so the steam can get to all the slices. The vegetables should not be piled deeper than 2–2 ½ inches. The depth will depend on the capacity of the pan used.
4. Details on amount of time each vegetable should be steam blanched, as well as other information, are given on the next page in chart form.

After blanching, the vegetables should be spread on the shelf for dehydrating. They must be placed in such a way as to allow adequate air circulation. Therefore, items such as potatoes, carrots, etc., should be placed one layer deep. However, items like parsley or shredded cabbage can be piled a little deeper and still have adequate air circulation.

Several varieties of vegetables may be placed in the dehydrator at one time, placing a different variety on each shelf and the stronger-smelling vegetables on the top shelves. Again, do not mix fruits and vegetables.

Storing Dehydrated Vegetables

When the vegetables are completely dry, remove trays from the dehydrator and loosen vegetables from netting. By the time the net is all loosened, the vegetables should be cool enough to place in storage containers. If not, let them cool a little longer. However,

Chart Number 7
Condensed Directions for Dehydrating Vegetables

It is not advisable to depend on any definite drying time for products. There are too many variables: the size of the load, the thickness of the slices, variations in temperature, the nature of the heat source, and the relative humidity of the air entering the dryer all are contributing factors. The timing in this table is a general guide only.

VEGETABLE	CONDITION	PREPARATION	Steaming Time Minutes*	Quantity Original Pounds	Quantity Dried Pounds	Average Drying Time: Hours
Asparagus	When tips are tender	Cut to green tips	5–8	50	3–4	7–9
Beans, Green, Snap	Mature but tender	Remove defective pods. Remove strings. Split lengthwise, or cut in 1 inch pieces, or french slice.	15–20	30	4–5	12–14
Beans, Lima	Mature but tender	Shell and wash	8–12	30 See Note 1	5–6	8–10
Beets, Small	Tender, good color	Wash, trim tops, but leave crown. After steaming, cool. Peel by hand, chill, slice in 3⁄16″ slices.	35–40 or until cooked	50	4–5	10–12
Broccoli	Good condition for table use	Trim, quarter stalks lengthwise. Wash.	8–12	50	5–6	12–15
Cabbage White or Red	Good for table use	Remove outer leaves; quarter head and core; cut into slices or shred.	5–6 or until wilted	56	3–4	10–12
Carrots	Very yellow; in good condition	Wash, trim, peel; cut into strips or slices 3⁄16″ thick	8–10	50	4–5	10–12
Cauliflower	Good for table use	Remove outer leaves, cut into individual section.	none	50	4–5	12–15

Product	Selection	Preparation				
Celery	Good for table use	Trim, wash, cut cross-wise into pieces 3/16" thick; use the leaves. (If celery is to be pulverized, do not steam)	2–4	50	2–3	12–15
Corn	In milk stage, sweet and tender.	Husk; steam on cob or dip in boiling water for 3 minutes until milk is set; cut off cob.	15–20 (on cob)	70	10	12–15
Cucumber	Mature and in good condition	Peel, cut in 3/16" slices	4–6	50	4–5	12–15
Mushrooms	Young; fresh. Gills pink; free from decay	Peel large ones; small ones do not require peeling. Use caps whole; slice stalks; discard woody ones	8–10			
Okra	Young pods	Wash, steam whole pod. Cut in 1" lengths	5–7	32	3	8–10
Onions and Garlic	Good condition for table use	Remove outer discolored layers. Slice or shred.	none	56	6–7	10–12
Peas See Note 2	Full grown, but before seeds begin to harden. Must be sweet and tender.	Shell, clean, and grade. Work quickly; peas lose quality and flavor when shelled.	10–15	30	2–3	8–10
Herbs	Mature, no wilted leaves	Wash quickly in cool water, shake off excess, and place on shelves.	none			4–6
Peppers-red, green	Sweet; in good condition	Wash. Clean out seeds. Slice 3/16" or cut in small pieces.	5–8	56	9–11	8–12
Peppers	Hot red	Wash; leave whole				
Potatoes	Good condition for table use	Wash, peel if desired, slice or dice. Rinse in cold water. Steam and rinse in cold water again.	4–6	56	9–11	8–12

(Continued)

Chart Number 7: (Continued)
Condensed Directions for Dehydrating Vegetables

VEGETABLE	CONDITION	PREPARATION	Steaming Time Minutes*	Quantity Original Pounds	Quantity Dried Pounds	Average Drying Time: Hours
Radishes	Good for table use	Wash, trim, cut into 3/16" slices		50	3	10–12
Soybeans	Edible and green. When pods are filled and beans are green and tender	Steam pods; then shell	5–7	30	3–4	6–8
Squash	Mature and in good condition	Wash; break into pieces. Peel; scrape off fiber and seeds. Cut into slices about 1/8" thick. Steam slices.	4–6	50	4–5	12–16
Spinach, Swiss Chard, Beet tops, etc.	Tender and crisp	Trim off roots. Wash. See that leaves are not wadded on trays. Loosen as drying progresses	4–6	50	2–3	8–10
Sweet Potatoes	Good condition for table use	Wash, steam, peel, and trim. Slice into 1/4" slices.	4–8	50	12–13	10–12
Tomatoes See Note 3	Firm, fully colored	Trim, wash, cut out top, slice into 3/16" slices and place on paper or cloth towels and pat to absorb maximum amount of moisture.	none	56	2–3	10–20
Turnip tops and other greens	Good condition for table use	Trim, sort and wash	7–8	50	3–4	8–10
Turnips and Rutabaga	Good condition for table use	Wash; peel; slice, dice or shred	10–12			

Powdered Vegetables	For use in soup or puree: Powder leafy vegetables after drying by grinding.
Soup Mixture	Cut vegetables into small pieces. Steam each kind separately until almost cooked. Do not steam onions. Dry. Combine and store. Satisfactory combinations may be made from cabbage, carrots, celery, corn, onions, and peas. Rice, dry beans, or split peas are usually added at the time of cooking.
1 Represents	Weight of beans and peas in pods
2 Peas	May be shelled by placing the pods in boiling water for 3 minutes. Remove from water and spread them on a wire screen with a mesh screen that is large enough to permit the shelled peas to pass through; have a receiving container underneath. Rub the pods vigorously over the screen with the hands; this action will burst the pods and empty them much more quickly than they can be shelled by hand.
3 See	Recipe for tomato paste
Beans and Peas	Those that have been allowed to dry on the vines should be given a short treatment in the drier (20–30 minutes). This drying will destroy insect eggs and bean weevils; it does however destroy the vitality of the product so it cannot be used for seed.
Vegetables	Those that are scalded will heat through and cook sufficiently in less time than those that are steamed. Steaming preserves vitamins to a greater extent and for that reason is recommended. The steaming time indicated on the table is an approximate one only; vegetables must be heated through, almost to the point of doneness.

Vegetables are dried when rigid and brittle.

When vegetables have been stored in a root cellar for a period of time, the starch starts to change to sugar. When these same vegetables are dehydrated, the drying time will be extended; the end product is completely satisfactory.

*This steaming time is for a 3-cup amount. If larger amounts are steamed, the steaming time should be extended a comparable amount.

Chart Number 8: Conversion chart
Fresh, Dehydrated, and Reconstituted Relationships: Vegetables

The following chart is provided as an aid in learning how to convert fresh vegetables to dehydrated and to reconstitute and use in recipes calling for either fresh or canned vegetables.

PRODUCT	THIS AMOUNT FRESH WEIGHT[1] POUNDS	YIELDS APPROXIMATELY THIS AMOUNT DEHYDRATED WEIGHT POUNDS	THIS AMOUNT DEHYDRATED CUPS	THIS AMOUNT DEHYDRATED Wt. Oz.	PLUS THIS AMOUNT WATER CUPS	YIELDS APPROXIMATELY THIS AMOUNT RECONSTITUTED CUPS	YIELDS APPROXIMATELY THIS AMOUNT RECONSTITUTED Wt.[2] Oz.	PLUS THIS MUCH LIQUID CUPS
Beans, Green	25	5	1	1.1	2	2 ¼	9.5	1
Beets, Red	25	3	1	1.9	2	2 ½	8.3	1 ⅓
Cabbage	25	1 ½	1	0.8	2	2	5.6	1 ¼
Carrots	25	3	1	2 ½	2	2 ¼	11.2	⅞
Celery	25	1 ½	1	1.3	2	2	6.8	1 ¼
Chard, Swiss	25		1	0.3	2	⅔	2.3	1 ⅔
Corn	25	3 ½	1	4.3	2	2	10.5	1 ⅛
Onions	25	2 ½	1	1.3	2	1 ⅔	7	1 ¼
Peas	25	2	1	3.9	2	2	11.6	1
Peppers, Green	25	4 ½	1	2	2	1 ⅓	11	1
Potatoes	25	5	1	2.9	2	1 ⅔	5.9	1 ½
Squash, Zucchini	25	2 ½	1	0.9	2	1	5.5	1 ⅓
Tomatoes	25	1 ½	1	1.3	2	1 ⅓	5.4	1 ⅓

[1] Ready to dehydrate, (peeled, etc.).
[2] Soaked for 3–3 ½ hours.

do not let the dehydrated vegetables stay on the shelves for any length of time, as they will start to absorb moisture and will have to be dehydrated again. Store immediately according to directions in the section "Storage after Dehydrating."

TESTING VEGETABLES FOR DRYNESS

It is sometimes necessary to test whether the vegetable is completely dried. The following guidelines are provided to simplify the task. (Remember to cool the piece of vegetable before testing.)

VEGETABLE	TESTS FOR DRYNESS
Beans, string and bush	Brittle
Beets	Tough; leathery
Broccoli	Brittle
Cabbage	Tough to brittle
Carrots	Tough to brittle
Cauliflower	Brittle
Celery	Tough to brittle
Corn (cut)	Dry; brittle
Cucumber	Brittle
Leaves for seasoning: celery, parsley, herbs	Brittle
Onions and garlic	Brittle; light-colored
Peas	Hard; wrinkled; will shatter when hit with a hammer
Peppers	Tough to brittle
Potatoes	Brittle
Pumpkin	Tough to brittle
Radishes	Brittle
Spinach, Swiss Chard, beet tops, etc.	Brittle
Squash	Tough to brittle
Sweet Potatoes	Brittle
Tomatoes	Leathery

DIRECTIONS FOR RECONSTITUTING DEHYDRATED VEGETABLES

General Rule: Use 1 cup dehydrated vegetables
2 cups hot water
Do not add salt

Soak vegetables for half an hour or longer until reconstituted, then cook on medium heat until vegetables are tender. At this point, add salt to taste and simmer for five minutes more. This rule applies to all vegetables.

"One cup dried vegetables is sufficient to serve four or five.

Two teaspoonfuls of dried powdered vegetables are sufficient for one cup water in making a puree, soup, or baby food. An exception is powdered or dried spinach, as it is very

Chart Number 9
Suggested Uses for Dehydrated Vegetables

For additional ideas, use your own imagination.

	Dehydrated-Powdered Add Water to Make Baby Food	Use in Main Dish	Soup	Vegetable Salad	Gelatin Salad	Side Dish
Beans, Green	x	x	x	x	x	x
Beets, Red	x	x		x	x	x
Cabbage	x	x	x			x
Carrots	x	x	x	x	x	x
Cauliflower		x	x			x
Celery		x	x			x
*Corn		x	x			x
Cucumbers	grind in blender and use powdered form					
Herbs	leave in larger pieces or grind and use in powdered form					
Onions & Garlic		x	x			
Peas	x	x	x	x		x
Peppers, Green		x	x	x		
Potatoes	x	x	x			x
Radishes				x	x	
Sweet Potatoes	x	x	x			x
Squash	x	x	x			x
Tomatoes		x	x			

* Grind corn in a wheat grinder to make cornmeal
All of the above vegetables can be ground and added in small quantities to provide additional flavor to other vegetables.

concentrated. Use from ½ to ¾ teaspoonful of it to each cup of water."[3] Simmer until cooked.

Powdered Dehydrated Vegetables

Vegetables can be powdered after they are dehydrated by pulverizing them in a blender. These can be used for purees, making soup, or baby food.

Powder onion, garlic, cucumbers, and celery and sprinkle on salads, casseroles, etc. Grind dehydrated corn in a wheat grinder to make excellent cornmeal.

Chart Number 10
Cost Conversion Chart: Vegetables

Multiply the item per pound cost by the factor figure. The result will be the cost of a gallon of dehydrated food. For example, if carrots cost 40 cents per pound, 40 cents × 20.8 equals $8.32 per gallon of dehydrated carrots.	
ITEM	FACTOR[1,2]
Beans, Green	5.5
Beets, Red	15.8
Cabbage	13.3
Carrots	20.8
Celery	21.6
Corn	30.7
Onions	13.0
Peas	48.0
Peppers, Green	11.1
Potatoes	14.5
Squash, Zucchini	9.0
Tomatoes	21.6

[1] This figure does not include any labor or container cost.
[2] This is only an approximate cost since there are a number of factors that can cause a small change in the figure.

[3]ref. *Ibid.*, pg. 80.

CHAPTER VIII
« DEHYDRATING HERBS »

Herbs are very easy to dehydrate. Wash them quickly in cool water, shake off excess water, and lay them on dehydrator shelves and dehydrate. This takes approximately 4–10 hours, depending on the herb. When dry, hold the herb by the stem with one hand and strip the dried leaves off the stem with the other hand directly into the storage jar.

USE HERBS FOR FLAVORING

The herbs listed below can be dried and used as spices and flavoring in cooking:

sage	dill	chives—chopped or snipped
bay leaf	celery tops	green onion tops—chopped or snipped
parsley	mint	

For additional herbs and their uses, refer to *The Herbalist*,[1] pg. 178–186.

From top left, clockwise: green onions, dill, mint, parsley.

[1]Joseph H. Meyer, *The Herbalist* (Clarence Meyer, 9th printing, 1972). This book gives many other uses for herbs that are interesting and useful.

Use Herbs for Tea

Try these herbs in your next cup of tea. Use one more teaspoon of herb or a combination of herbs than the number of persons to be served. Pour in the correct amount of boiling water and let steep for three minutes. Stir, and after another minute, pour into cups.

spearmint	alfalfa	cinnamon
catnip	bay leaf	ginger
rose hips	parsley	peppermint

For additional herbs and directions, refer to *The Herbalist*, pg. 166–177.

Use Herbs for Sachets

The following can be dehydrated to use in making fragrant sachets. Place desired dehydrated mixtures or a single fragrance in a closed jar for at least six weeks and then put in a small cloth bag for use.

lavender	rosemary	violet
rose petals	sandalwood	cloves
hollyhock	orange	mint

For additional fragrances, refer to *The Herbalist*, pg. 196–203.

Dried flowers make excellent additions to potpourri baskets and sachets.

CHAPTER IX

« DEHYDRATING MEATS »

Beef jerky.

JERKY AND STEW MEAT

There are two purposes for dehydrating meats and the end use dictates which of the two methods of preparation is used.

The first method is for making jerky, which is dried and seasoned meat that is eaten in its dry state and not reconstituted or cooked. Therefore, caution must be used to make sure the meat is taken from healthy animals that do not contain worms, etc. Recipes for this method are found in the recipe section and should be followed carefully.

The second method of dehydrating meat is for using it in soups, stews, and main dishes. Experimentation has proven that meats that are to be reconstituted must be cooked before dehydrating to insure reconstitution to a tender, palatable end product.

Note: Dehydrated meat that is not cooked before dehydrating cannot be reconstituted. It will remain tough and chewy, much like jerky, even after many hours of cooking.

Chicken, turkey, rabbit, and beef must be cooked to a done, but tender, state before they are sliced, diced, chipped, or stripped for drying. Cut it ready for your personal recipes, making sure all fat is removed. The fat is easier to see and remove when the cooked meat is chilled. Fat becomes rancid and very unpleasant to the taste when stored without refrigeration. The cooked, dehydrated meat will be quite crisp when dry enough to store.

The same preparation can be used for game animals and birds.

The storage life of cooked and dehydrated meat is shorter than that of fruits and vegetables. Follow the same storage directions and keep dehydrated meat in air-tight containers in a cool, dark place.

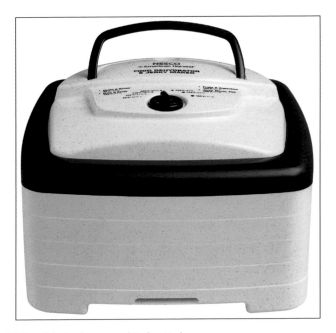

Nesco FD-80 Food Dehydrator and Jerky Maker.
© The Metal Ware Corporation.

CHAPTER X
« STORAGE AFTER DEHYDRATING »

COOL, DARK, AND DRY: KEYS TO SUCCESSFUL STORAGE

There are three things to remember when storing dehydrated foods: cool, dark, and dry. By remembering these things, food will keep for a long time with little loss of food value. The following are descriptions of the best conditions, although not everyone will be able to achieve them. However, try to come as close as possible to these rules for food storage.

Cool: The storage temperature should be 60°F or below if possible. Foods have a browning rate, or rate at which they discolor or turn brown. This browning rate doubles for each 12–15°F in temperature rise.

Dark: This can be easily accomplished through one of the following methods: If you have a storeroom with a window, the window should be covered to keep out the light; any other opening that might admit light should also be covered. If a storeroom is not available, black plastic or material can be hung in front of the shelves to eliminate the light. Jars of food may be wrapped in newspaper or black plastic.

We talked with a woman who had kept bottled fruit for twenty years in her ranch home in the mountains; the conditions were ideal and the fruit was still light in color and tasted delicious.

Dry: Keep dehydrated food in air-tight containers or the food will absorb moisture and spoil. You may use plastic cooking pouches and seal them with a commercially-sold heat sealer. You may also use glass jars or large metal cans if the lids are air-tight. We suggest putting large plastic bags in the cans first and then placing the food inside. Tie the tops of the plastic bags and put the can lids on tight.

There are now a number of large plastic storage containers on the market. Our experience so far has indicated that some of these are adequate for storing dehydrated food. However, you must make sure they are of food-grade plastic and are moisture-tight. Containers should be filled as full as is possible in order to displace air. Amounts for single meals may be put into individual plastic bags and stored tightly in larger containers so the product is not exposed to the air unnecessarily.

Extreme cold will not injure dehydrated products because they are practically free from water.

We also suggest using a desiccant inside the containers. The desiccant absorbs moisture and the dehydrated food will last two to three times longer than dehydrated food stored without using the desiccant.

It is best not to store cans or bottles directly on cement floors; a low riser made with 2' × 4's is inexpensive, efficient, and movable.

Examine the food occasionally. If there is any sign of moisture, spread the product on shelves and dehydrate until all evidence of moisture is removed.

CHAPTER XI
« BREAD RECIPES »

« APRICOT NUT BREAD »

Yield: 1 loaf

1 cup dehydrated diced apricots	½ teaspoon salt
1 cup water	2 eggs, beaten lightly
milk	¾ cup sugar
2 ½ cups all-purpose flour	2 tablespoons melted shortening
3 teaspoons double-acting baking powder	½ cup chopped nuts

1. Soak apricots in water until reconstituted.
2. Grease a 9 × 5 × 3-inch loaf pan and line neatly with waxed paper.
3. Sift together the flour, baking powder, and salt.
4. Gradually beat together eggs and sugar.
5. Drain liquid from apricots, add enough milk to liquid to equal 1 cup, then put liquid into 3-quart mixing bowl.
6. Stir together egg mixture, shortening, and drained apricots, then add to flour mixture and nuts and beat well.
7. Pour into prepared pan. Let stand 10 minutes, then cover with another pan of same size and place in a 350°F oven. Bake for 20 minutes, then uncover and bake for 50 minutes longer or until loaf tests done.
8. Remove from pan to cake rack to cool before slicing.

« BANANA BREAD »

Yield: 1 large loaf or 2 small loaves

2 cups dehydrated bananas	1 teaspoon salt
2 cups warm water	3 tablespoons vegetable oil
2 ½ cups sifted flour	¾ cup milk
1 cup sugar	1 egg
3 ½ teaspoons baking powder	1 cup finely chopped nuts

1. Soak bananas in warm water until reconstituted, then drain.
2. Cream together flour, sugar, baking powder, salt, vegetable oil, milk, egg, and reconstituted bananas.
3. Mix thoroughly; beat on medium speed for half a minute, scraping side and bottom of bowl constantly. When thoroughly mixed, add the nuts.
4. Pour into greased and floured 9 × 5 × 3-inch loaf pan or two 8 ½ × 4 ½ × 2 ½-inch loaf pans.
5. Bake in a 350°F oven 55–65 minutes or until wooden pick inserted in center comes out clean.
6. Remove from pan; cool thoroughly before slicing.

« BANANA DOUGHNUTS »

Yield: about 42

¾ cup dehydrated bananas
1 cup water
5 cups all-purpose flour
3 teaspoons baking powder
1 teaspoon baking soda
2 teaspoons salt

1 teaspoon nutmeg
¼ cup shortening
1 cup sugar
1 ½ teaspoons vanilla
3 eggs, well beaten
½ cup buttermilk

1. Soak bananas in water for half an hour.
2. Sift together flour, baking powder, baking soda, salt, and nutmeg.
3. Cream the shortening, then blend in and beat until light and fluffy the sugar, vanilla, and beaten eggs. Beat mixture well for 2 minutes.
4. Stir in and thoroughly mix the drained reconstituted bananas and buttermilk.
5. Add flour mixture in 3 or 4 portions, stirring just enough to mix after each addition. Chill dough before rolling.
6. Remove one-fourth of dough from refrigerator at a time, knead it lightly 4 or 5 times, roll out on floured pastry cloth to ⅜" thickness, and cut with floured 2 ½" doughnut cutter.
7. Fry in deep fat heated to 350°F until golden brown, then lift out and drain on absorbent paper. If desired, the dough may be covered tightly and kept in the refrigerator for 1 or 2 days, to be fried as needed.

« SPICY BANANA NUT BREAD »

Yield: 1 loaf

1 cup dehydrated bananas
1 cup water
⅓ cup shortening
⅔ cup sugar
1 teaspoon vanilla extract
1 ¾ cups all-purpose flour

2 teaspoons baking powder
½ teaspoon salt
1 teaspoon cinnamon
⅛ teaspoon cardamom
⅛ teaspoon mace
½ cup chopped nuts

1. Soak bananas in water until reconstituted.
2. Cream together until light and fluffy the shortening and sugar, then add in the vanilla extract. Beat mixture well.
3. Sift together the flour, baking powder, salt, cinnamon, cardamom, and mace.
4. In turns, add the reconstituted bananas and the creamed mixture to the sifted dry ingredients. When all ingredients have been added, stir in the nuts.
5. Grease bottom of 9 ¼ × 5 ¼ × 2 ¾-inch loaf pan. Pour batter into pan.
6. Bake in 350°F oven for 60–70 minutes. Serve warm or cold at any meal.

Yield: 8–10 muffins

1 cup dehydrated bananas	3 tablespoons sugar
1 cup water	2 small eggs
1 ½ cups all-purpose flour	¼ teaspoon grated lemon rind
1 ¼ teaspoons baking powder	1 teaspoon lemon juice
½ teaspoon baking soda	3 tablespoons buttermilk
1 teaspoon salt	3 tablespoons shortening

1. Preheat oven to 400°F and grease an 8–10-cup medium muffin pan.
2. Soak bananas in water until reconstituted.
3. Sift together flour, baking powder, baking soda, salt, and sugar.
4. Beat eggs, then add in the reconstituted bananas. When mixed, add in the lemon rind, lemon juice, buttermilk, and shortening. Mix thoroughly.
5. Add liquid mixture all at once to dry ingredients; stir quickly and vigorously until flour is just dampened, but no more.
6. Spoon batter into prepared pans and place in preheated oven.
7. Bake about 30 minutes or until well-browned. Serve hot.

« BANANA WAFFLES »

Yield: six 7-inch waffles

1 cup dehydrated bananas
1 cup water
2 cups all-purpose flour
3 teaspoons baking powder
1 tablespoon sugar

¾ teaspoon salt
3 eggs
1 ½ cups milk
⅓ cup melted shortening

1. Soak bananas in water until reconstituted, then drain.
2. Sift together flour, baking powder, sugar, and salt.
3. Beat eggs, then add in milk and melted shortening. When mixed, pour into dry ingredients.
4. Add reconstituted bananas and beat mixture until smooth.
5. Using ½ cup batter for each waffle, bake in a hot waffle iron until golden brown.
6. Serve immediately with butter, hot syrup, powdered sugar, or pureed fruit.

« CORNMEAL PANCAKES »

Yield: approximately twenty 4-inch pancakes

¾ cup cornmeal
1 cup boiling water
1 cup buttermilk
2 eggs

1 cup whole wheat or white flour
1 tablespoon baking powder
1 teaspoon salt
¼ cup cooking oil

1. Grind one cup dehydrated corn in a wheat grinder. This will equal ¾ cup cornmeal.
2. Mix all ingredients thoroughly, then cook on hot griddle.

Note: Cornmeal pancakes will take longer to cook as cornmeal takes longer to cook then flour.

« CORN BREAD »

1 cup whole wheat or white flour
¼ cup white or brown sugar
4 teaspoons baking powder
¾ teaspoon salt
1 cup cornmeal

1 cup milk or buttermilk
¼ cup liquid shortening
1 egg yolk
2 egg whites

A plate of corn bread is perfect for any meal.

1. Grind 1 ⅓ cups dehydrated corn in wheat grinder. This will yield 1 cup cornmeal.
2. Mix together flour, sugar, baking powder, salt, and cornmeal.
3. Add milk or buttermilk, liquid shortening, and egg yolk. Beat mixture until smooth.
4. Beat egg whites until they are stiff, then fold into batter.
5. Pour into greased 8 × 8 × 2-inch pan and bake in preheated oven 425°F for 20–25 minutes.

« CRUNCHY FRIED CORN CAKES »

Yield: 8 cakes

1 ½ cups cornmeal	1 ½ cups boiling water
¾ teaspoon salt	⅓ cup shortening

1. Grind 2 cups dehydrated corn in a wheat grinder. This will yield 1 ½ cups cornmeal.
2. Put cornmeal and salt into a mixing bowl and slowly add in boiling water, beating mixture as you do until you have a smooth batter stiff enough to shape.
3. Mold batter neatly into flat oval cakes.
4. Heat shortening in a 10-inch skillet until the shortening is sizzling but not smoking hot. Lay cakes in and fry quickly, until each side is a rich golden brown; roughly 3 to 4 minutes. Don't turn cakes until this rich color develops. Serve with butter.

« HUSH PUPPIES »

Yield: 4–5 servings

⅓ cup all-purpose flour
3 teaspoons baking powder
1 teaspoon salt
1 ¾ cups cornmeal

2 tablespoons reconstituted onion
½ cup plus 1 tablespoon buttermilk
½ cup tomato juice

1. Grind 2 ¼ cups dehydrated corn in a wheat grinder. This will yield 1 ¾ cups cornmeal.
2. Sift together flour, baking powder, salt, and cornmeal. Add in reconstituted onion.
3. Beat together buttermilk and tomato juice, then pour liquid into dry ingredients and beat well until blended.
4. Mixture should be a drop batter. Melt enough shortening in a frying kettle or deep skillet to measure 2 ½ inches deep. Heat frying kettle or skillet to 380°F.
5. Fry 6–8 hush puppies at a time. To drop batter into hot fat, dip teaspoon first into hot fat, then into batter.
6. Fry to rich golden brown on the bottom before flipping hush puppies over. When brown and done all the way through, lift out onto paper towels to drain. Cover with paper towels until all of the batter has been fried. Serve very hot.

« PRUNE NUT BREAD »

Yield: 1 loaf

1 cup uncooked dehydrated prunes or
　plums
½ cup orange juice
½ cup hot water
½ teaspoon grated orange rind
2 cups all-purpose flour
3 teaspoons baking powder

½ teaspoon salt
½ teaspoon cinnamon
¾ cup sugar
1 tablespoon melted shortening
2 beaten eggs
½ cup chopped nuts

1. Grease an 8 × 4 × 2 ½-inch loaf pan.
2. Chop prunes into bite-sized pieces, and then pour over them the orange juice, hot water, and grated orange rind. Let mixture stand for 10 minutes, then add melted shortening and beaten eggs.
3. Sift together flour, baking powder, salt, cinnamon, and sugar, then add to prune mixture. Mix thoroughly.
4. When wet and dry ingredients have been mixed, stir in chopped nuts.
5. Pour into prepared pan and bake in a 350°F oven for 1 hour or until loaf tests done. Remove from pan to cake rack to cool.

Yield: 5 servings

2 ¼ cups milk
2 tablespoons butter
1 teaspoon salt

⅔ cup yellow cornmeal
3 eggs, separating yolks and whites

1. Grind 1 cup of dehydrated corn in a wheat grinder. This will equal ⅔ cup resulting cornmeal.
2. Heat to the milk to scalding, then add in the butter, salt, and cornmeal.
3. Boil gently for one minute, stirring constantly.
4. Remove from heat and cool for 5 minutes, before stirring in well-beaten egg yolks.
5. Beat egg whites until stiff, then fold into the mixture.
6. Pour into a greased 5-cup casserole dish. Bake at 355°F for 35–40 minutes. Serve spooned from baking dish with butter.

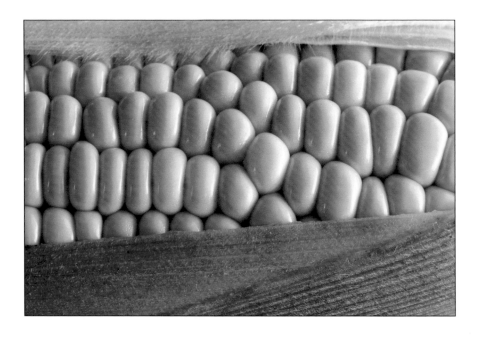

CHAPTER XII
« CAKE RECIPES »

« APPLE CRUMB CAKE »

2 cups dehydrated apples
2 cups water
1 cup oatmeal
1 cup flour

½ cup brown sugar
½ teaspoon baking soda
½ cup margarine or butter (1 stick)

1. Soak apples in water until reconstituted, then drain.
2. Mix together the oatmeal, flour, brown sugar, baking soda, and margarine (or butter) until crumbly.
3. Pat half of mixture in bottom of 8 × 8-inch pan. Spread apples over top of crumbly mixture. Sprinkle with sugar and cinnamon and cover with remaining crumbs.
4. Bake in a 350°F oven for 1 hour. Serve warm or cold with scoop of ice cream.

Note: Reconstituted dehydrated peaches, apricots, or prunes may be substituted for the apples.

« APPLE UPSY-DAISY CAKE »

2 cups dehydrated apples
2 cups water
½ cup sugar

1 cup firmly packed light brown sugar
1 teaspoon cinnamon
1 spice cake mix

1. Soak apples in water until reconstituted, then cook the apples until they are completely tender; drain and reserve liquid.
2. Add in sugar. Stir until sugar is dissolved, then mash apples and add enough reserved liquid until the mixture has the consistency of applesauce.
3. Combine mashed apples with brown sugar and cinnamon.
4. Spread evenly in bottom of greased 13 × 9 × 2-inch oblong pan.
5. Mix according to directions on the spice cake mix.

6. Pour batter carefully over applesauce layer. Bake approximately 35 minutes at 350°F.

7. Remove to serving plate and spoon applesauce mixture from bottom of pan evenly over top of cake. Serve warm, topped with whipped cream or ice cream.

« APPLESAUCE DATE CAKE »

1 ½ cups dehydrated apples
2 cups warm water
½ cup sugar
½ teaspoon lemon juice
¼ cup shortening
½ teaspoon salt
1 egg

1 ½ cups sifted flour
1 teaspoon baking soda
½ teaspoon cinnamon
½ teaspoon cloves
½ cup chopped nuts
½ cup chopped dates

1. Soak apples in water until reconstituted, then simmer for 15 minutes.
2. Stir in sugar and lemon juice and cook to your desired applesauce thickness.
3. Cream together the shortening, salt, and egg.
4. Sift the flour, baking soda, cinnamon, and cloves.
5. Add applesauce alternately with sifted dry ingredients, mixing well, then stir in nuts and dates.
6. Pour batter into 6 × 10 × 2-inch pan which has been lightly greased and dusted with flour. Bake in 350°F oven for 35–40 minutes. Allow to cool before frosting.

Note: Reconstitute dehydrated peaches, apricots, or prunes and put through food grinder to make a thick puree of applesauce consistency and substitute for the apples.

« GERMAN DUTCH APPLE CAKE »

3 cups dehydrated apples
3 cups water
2 large eggs
1 cup vegetable oil
2 cups sugar
2 cups flour

1 teaspoon baking soda
1 ½ teaspoons water
1 teaspoon cinnamon
1 cup chopped nuts

1. Soak apples in water until reconstituted, then drain.
2. Mix together until foamy the eggs and vegetable oil, then add in the sugar, flour, baking soda, cinnamon, and 1 ½ teaspoons of water.
3. Mix together the drained apples and nuts, then add to the batter. Mix thoroughly, then spread in oblong pan.
4. Bake at 350°F for 50–60 minutes.

« ICING »

1 package (3 ounces) cream cheese
1 teaspoon melted butter
¼ teaspoon vanilla
1 cup powdered sugar

Mix together the ingredients and spread over warm German Dutch Apple Cake.

« APPLE COFFEE CAKE »

Yield: 10–15 servings

3 cups dehydrated apples
3 cups water
3 ½ cups all-purpose flour
1 cup milk
1 package dry granulated yeast
¼ cup lukewarm water
1 teaspoon sugar

⅓ cup shortening
1 teaspoon salt
1 ⅔ cups and 1 teaspoon sugar
3 eggs, beaten
1 teaspoon vanilla extract
2 teaspoons cinnamon

1. Sift the flour.
2. Soak apples in water until reconstituted, then drain.
3. Scald milk on top of double boiler and pour into 3-quart mixing bowl to cool to lukewarm.
4. Crumble the yeast into the lukewarm water. Stir in 1 teaspoon sugar and let soften for 10 minutes.
5. Stir yeast mixture into scaled milk and beat in 1 ½ cups of the flour. Beat mixture until smooth, then cover and let rise in warm place until light, about 45 minutes.
6. Cream together in another bowl the shortening, salt, and ⅔ cup of sugar. Gradually add in yeast batter, stirring to mix well. Beat into the batter eggs and vanilla extract. Add remaining flour and beat until thoroughly mixed.
7. Spread into 2 well-greased pans 11 × 7 × 1 ½-inch or two 10-inch round layer cake pans.
8. Pat dough with melted butter; lay drained apples close together, pressing slightly into batter.
9. Sprinkle the cinnamon and the remainder of the sugar evenly over apples.
10. Cover, let rise in a warm place until double, about 1 hour. Cover pan with an inverted second pan of same size to thoroughly cook apples.
11. Bake 10 minutes in 400°F oven, then remove covers and bake about 20 minutes longer or until apples are tender and cakes are done. Serve warm.

« RAW APPLE CAKE »

Yield: one 8 × 12-inch cake

2 ½ cups dehydrated apples
2 ½ cups water
½ cup shortening
1 cup sugar
2 cups sifted flour
1 ½ tablespoons cocoa
2 teaspoons baking soda
1 teaspoon salt

1 teaspoon cinnamon
1 teaspoon nutmeg
1 teaspoon allspice
1 cup chopped dates
1 cup chopped walnuts
½ cup candied cherries (optional)
1 ½ cups glazed mixed fruits (optional)

1. Soak apples in water until reconstituted, then drain.
2. Cream together the shortening and sugar, then mix in the drained apples.
3. Sift the flour, cocoa, baking soda, salt, cinnamon, nutmeg, and allspice together, then stir into the drained apple mixture.
4. Add the dates and walnuts to the batter. If you would like, add in the cherries and glazed mixed fruits.
5. Spread batter in a greased and floured 8 × 12-inch cake pan and bake at 325°F for 1 hour.
6. Remove from oven and spread on topping. Place cake under broiler for 5 minutes or until glazed.

Note: This is a good holiday season cake as it keeps well.

« TOPPING »

¼ cup melted butter or margarine
1 cup powdered sugar
½ orange: juice and grated rind

1. Blend together the butter or margarine with the powdered sugar, then stir in orange juice and rind.
2. Spread on hot cake.

« APRICOT UPSIDE-DOWN CAKE »

Yield: 4–6 servings

1 cup dehydrated apricots
1 cup water or milk
⅓ cup butter or margarine
½ cup packed brown sugar
3 tablespoons white corn syrup
1 cup all-purpose flour

1 ¼ teaspoons baking powder
¼ teaspoon salt
¼ cup shortening
½ cup sugar
2 eggs
¼ teaspoon almond extract

1. Preheat oven to 350°F.
2. Soak the apricots in water until reconstituted. Drain the apricots, reserving the juice. There should be ¼ cup of juice; if not, add enough milk to make ¼ cup.

3. Put in sauce pan over low heat butter or margarine and brown sugar. Stir together and cook until mixture just begins to bubble. Add in corn syrup, then remove pan from heat. Pour mixture into an 8 × 8 × 2-inch pan and arrange apricot halves cut-side up in sugar-butter mixture.
4. Sift together flour, baking powder, and salt.
5. Cream together shortening and sugar. Beat in eggs, one at a time until smooth, then add in almond extract.
6. Using a wooden spoon, stir in flour and liquid alternately, beating until smooth after each addition. Spoon batter carefully over apricots, then spread out gently.
7. Bake for 35 minutes or until cake tests done. Cool on cake rack 10 minutes, then invert onto serving plate, pouring the juice over the cake. Serve warm; plain or with whipped cream.

« BANANA-NUT LAYER CAKE »

Yield: 10–12 servings

⅔ cup dehydrated bananas
1 cup water
1 ¾ cups cake flour or 1 ½ cups
    all-purpose flour
1 teaspoon soda
½ teaspoon baking salt
1 teaspoon lemon juice

½ cup buttermilk
½ cup shortening
1 cup sugar
2 eggs
1 teaspoon vanilla
⅓ cup finely-chopped nuts

1. Soak bananas in water for half an hour, then drain.
2. Grease two 8-inch layer pans; line bottoms with greased waxed paper. Preheat oven to 350°F.
3. Sift together four times the cake or all-purpose flour, baking soda, and salt.
4. Mash the drained bananas to a fine paste, then add the lemon juice and buttermilk.
5. Cream together the shortening and sugar, then add the eggs, one at a time, and beat after each addition. Stir in vanilla.
6. Add dry ingredients alternately with banana mixture, beginning and ending with flour, beating mixture well with each addition. When batter is fully mixed, fold in the nuts.
7. Pour batter into prepared pans. Bake 28–30 minutes. Remove to cake racks and cool in pans 8–10 minutes, then turn cakes out on racks. Loosen the waxed paper but leave it on cakes.
8. When cakes are fully cool, flip cakes over and put layers together with whipped cream topping.

« WHIPPED CREAM TOPPING »

Yield: 10–12 servings

½ pint whipping cream
2 tablespoons powdered sugar
½ teaspoon vanilla

1. Chill bowl and rotary beater in refrigerator.
2. Whip whipping cream, powered sugar, and vanilla until stiff.
3. Place one layer of cake on serving plate bottom-side up. Spread with whipped cream. Now carefully place second layer top-side up on cream filling and spread rest of whipped cream on top and sides.
4. Serve promptly, storing leftover cake in refrigerator.

« BANANA-NUT CUPCAKES »

Follow recipe for Banana-Nut Layer Cake (pg. 78)

1. Spoon batter into greased muffin pans with 15–16 medium cups, filling cups a little more than half full, or use paper cups.
2. Bake in 375°F oven for 15–18 minutes, or until cakes test done.
3. Cool in pans on cake racks 5 minutes, then remove to racks to finish cooling.

« CARROT CAKE »

1 ½ cups dehydrated carrots
3 cups cold water
1 cup white sugar
1 cup brown sugar, firmly packed
2 cups flour
1 ¼ teaspoons baking soda
1 teaspoon salt

1 teaspoon baking powder
2 teaspoons cinnamon
2 cups vegetable oil
4 beaten eggs
1 cup chopped nuts
1 cup raisins
1 cup chocolate chips

1. Soak carrots in water until they are their normal size, then drain. Grind reconstituted carrots in a food grinder, or push through grater.
2. Thoroughly mix white sugar, brown sugar, flour, baking soda, salt, baking powder, and cinnamon.

3. Add the vegetable oil, eggs, ground carrots, nuts, raisins, and chocolate chips and mix well.
4. Pour batter into 2 greased loaf pans or a 9 × 13-inch baking pan. Bake cake at 325°F one hour or until done.

« FROSTING FOR CARROT CAKE »

1 package (8 ounces) cream cheese, softened
½ stick butter (¼ cup) or margarine
2 teaspoons vanilla

1 box (1 pound) powdered sugar
½ cup chopped pecans (optional)
1 cup coconut (optional)

1. Beat together the cream cheese and butter or margarine until fluffy. Add in the vanilla and powdered sugar.
2. Beat mixture until fluffy and of spreading consistency, then frost layers and sides of cake.
3. If desired, sprinkle with a mixture of ½ cup chopped pecans and 1 cup coconut between layers and on top.

« CHERRY COFFEE CAKE »

Yield: 10–15 servings

3 cups dehydrated pie cherries
3 cups water

Follow recipe for Apple Coffee Cake (pg. 75–76), except use drained reconstituted cherries instead of apples and sprinkle ¾ to 1 cup sugar evenly over the fruit.

« PEACH COFFEE CAKE »

Yield: 10–15 servings

3 cups dehydrated peaches
3 cups water

Follow recipe for Apple Coffee Cake (pg. 75–76), except use drained reconstituted peaches instead of apples and sprinkle ¾ to 1 cup sugar evenly over the fruit.

1 cup dehydrated rhubarb
2 cups warm water
½ cup shortening
1 ½ cups brown sugar
1 beaten egg

1 cup buttermilk
2 cups sifted flour
1 teaspoon baking soda
½ cup white sugar
1 teaspoon cinnamon

1. Soak the rhubarb in water until reconstituted, then cook covered until almost tender. When almost tender, drain.
2. Cream together shortening and brown sugar, then add in beaten egg. Add in buttermilk, flour, and baking soda, alternately.
3. Lightly fold the drained rhubarb into the batter, then spread batter in a greased and floured pan.
4. Sprinkle top with sugar and cinnamon and bake at 350°F for 30–35 minutes.

CHAPTER XIII
« CEREAL AND COOKIE RECIPES »

« PREPARED CEREAL »

16 cups quick-cooking oats
2 cups coconut
1 cup wheat germ
2 cups raw sugar

3 cups whole wheat flour (fresh ground)
1 cup vegetable oil
1 ½ tablespoons salt
½ cup honey

1. Stir together the oats, coconut, wheat germ, and raw sugar.
2. Mix together the wheat flour, vegetable oil, salt, and honey and pour over dry ingredients.
3. Mix together with hands until crumbly. Bake 2 hours at 250°F, stirring every half hour.
4. Keep enough cereal for a week in the refrigerator and freeze the rest.

Note: You may add the following: pecans, raisins, dehydrated apples, dehydrated apricots, bananas, dehydrated Bing cherries, dates, or blueberries.

« GLAZED FRESH APPLE COOKIES »

Yield: 5 dozen

¾ cup dehydrated apples
1 cup water
½ cup shortening
1 ⅓ cups brown sugar
1 egg
2 cups sifted all-purpose flour

1 teaspoon baking soda
½ teaspoon salt
1 teaspoon cinnamon
½ teaspoon nutmeg
1 teaspoon ground cloves
¼ cup apple juice or milk

1. Soak apples in water and let stand until apples have absorbed most of the water.
2. Cream together the shortening, brown sugar, and egg.
3. Sift together the flour, baking soda, salt, cinnamon, nutmeg, and cloves.

4. Add half of the dry ingredients to shortening, sugar, and egg mixture. Mix thoroughly. Add apple juice to this mixture and blend well.
5. Add the rest of the dry ingredients and the apple mixture to the batter and mix well.
6. Drop by teaspoonful on greased cookie sheet. Bake at 400°F for 10–12 minutes. Frost while hot with vanilla glaze.

« VANILLA GLAZE »

1 ½ cups powdered sugar
2 ½ tablespoons apple juice or cream
½ teaspoon salt

¼ teaspoon vanilla
1 tablespoon butter

1. Mix all ingredients well and frost cookies while hot.

CHAPTER XIV
« DESSERT RECIPES »

« APPLE BETTY »

1 ½ cups dehydrated cooking apples
3 cups water
2 cups soft bread crumbs
⅓ cup brown sugar

1 teaspoon cinnamon
¼ cup and ½ tablespoon melted butter
¾ cup water drained from apples

1. Mix together the apples and water and simmer until tender. Drain, reserving liquid.
2. Combine 1 ½ cups of bread crumbs, brown sugar, and cinnamon and put in buttered casserole dish. Mix in the drained reconstituted apples.
3. Pour over mixture in casserole dish ¼ cup melted butter and the reserved liquid.
4. Mix together ½ cup bread crumbs with the left of the melted butter and sprinkle over top of dish.
5. Bake at 350°F for 30–45 minutes.

Note: Blueberries are delicious to use in this recipe in place of apples.

« APPLE BROWNIES »

Yield: 16 brownies

1 cup dehydrated apples
2 cups water
½ cup shortening
2 squares unsweetened chocolate
1 cup sugar
½ teaspoon vanilla
2 eggs, beaten

1 cup sifted flour
1 teaspoon baking powder
½ teaspoon salt
1 teaspoon cinnamon
½ teaspoon mace
½ cup chopped nuts
½ cup chopped dates

1. Mix together the apples and water and let sit until water is almost absorbed or until apples have become a normal size. Drain.
2. Melt together the shortening and chocolate. When melted, beat in the sugar and vanilla, then stir in the eggs.

3. Sift together the flour, baking powder, salt, cinnamon, and mace. Stir the sifted mixture into the other ingredients.
4. Mix in the drained apples, nuts, and dates.
5. Spread batter in a greased 9-inch square pan. Bake at 350°F 30–35 minutes. Cut while warm into 2-inch squares.

« APPLE FLUFF »

1 cup dehydrated apples
2 cups water
1 cup sugar
½ teaspoon salt
1 teaspoon baking soda
½ cup shortening
1 egg, beaten

1 ½ cup flour
1 teaspoon cinnamon
1 teaspoon baking powder
½ cup brown sugar
½ cup chopped nuts
½ teaspoon cinnamon

1. Reconstitute apples in water. Simmer over low heat until tender, then drain.
2. Cream together the sugar, salt, baking soda, shortening, and egg.
3. Sift together the flour, cinnamon, and baking powder. Add sifted mixture to creamed ingredients.
4. Add the reconstituted apples and mix together. Spread batter in 9-inch square pan and sprinkle with brown sugar, nuts, and cinnamon. Bake at 325°F for 45 minutes.

Note: Use reconstituted dehydrated peaches, apricots, or prunes in place of the apples.

« APPLE FRITTERS »

1 cup dehydrated apples
1 cup water
1 cup all-purpose flour
1 teaspoon baking powder
½ teaspoon salt

3 tablespoons sugar
⅓ cup milk
1 teaspoon melted butter
1 egg

1. Soak apples in water until reconstituted, then drain. Cut apples into bite-sized pieces.
2. Sift together the flour, baking powder, salt, and sugar.
3. Beat the egg, adding in the milk and melted butter. Mix together, then add in the flour mixture and beat to a smooth batter. Fold in the reconstituted apples.
4. In a 3-quart frying kettle, heat shortening to 350°F. No frying basket is needed for fritters.
5. Dip spoon into hot fat and quickly dip up a heaping teaspoon of batter, and with a second spoon quickly push it into the fat. Work quickly so 6 or 7 fritters can fry at the same time. Temperature drops quite fast but try to maintain it around 350°F throughout frying.
6. Turn fritters when brown on underside. It requires 4–5 minutes to fry fritters of this size to a golden brown and to cook all the way through. Lift out quickly with food fork or slotted spoon onto paper towels to drain.
7. Serve hot like pancakes with sugar or syrup, or serve sprinkled with powdered sugar for dessert.

Hint: To save fat, strain while hot through one layer of paper towels or cheesecloth placed in a coarse sieve over a shortening or coffee can. Cool. Store fat in refrigerator for later usage.
Note: Fritters come out fat or flat, depending on the way you fry them; in deep fat they come out globular, in shallow fat they come out flat. They are good either way.

« APPLE PANDOWDY »

5 cups dehydrated apples
5 cups water
½ cup sugar

¼ teaspoon nutmeg
¼ teaspoon salt

1. Preheat oven to 350°F.
2. Soak apples in water until reconstituted.
3. Butter bottom and sides of an 8 × 8 × 2-inch baking pan. Spread drained reconstituted apples in a uniform layer over bottom of pan. Quickly sift ¼ teaspoon salt over them to prevent discoloration, then sprinkle on sugar and nutmeg.
4. Cover and place in oven for 10 minutes while preparing the batter below.

« COTTAGE PUDDING BATTER »

1 ¾ cups all-purpose flour
2 teaspoons baking powder
¼ teaspoon salt
¼ teaspoon baking soda
⅓ cup soft butter, margarine, or
    shortening

⅔ cup sugar
1 egg
1 teaspoon vanilla
1 cup buttermilk

1. Sift together the flour, baking powder, salt, and baking soda.
2. Cream until smooth butter, margarine, or shortening, then gradually add in the sugar, creaming well. Add egg and beat until fluffy.
3. Add vanilla and buttermilk alternately with flour mixture, beating till smooth after each addition.
4. Remove pan with apples in it and quickly spread batter evenly over hot apples. Bake 30–35 minutes or until pudding tests done. Remove to cake rack to cool 5 minutes, then loosen sides and invert onto serving plate.
5. Serve warm with Apple Pandowdy.

« SOFT HARD SAUCE »

½ cup butter
1 teaspoon vanilla or
    ½ teaspoon almond extract

dash of salt
1 ⅓ cups powdered sugar

1. Cream butter, then add in vanilla or almond extract. When mixed, add in the salt and powdered sugar.
2. Mixture should be fairly stiff when finished.

« CHEESE APPLE CRISP »

Yield: 6 servings

3 cups dehydrated apples
3 cups warm water
¾ cup brown sugar
¼ cup nonfat dry milk
⅓ cup all-purpose flour

¼ cup rolled oats
½ teaspoon cinnamon
⅛ teaspoon salt
¼ cup butter or margarine
1 cup shredded cheese

1. Reconstitute apples in warm water. Let sit 30 minutes, then drain.
2. Combine brown sugar, nonfat dry milk, flour, oats, cinnamon, and salt in a bowl. Add butter or margarine and chees and work in until crumbly.

3. Arrange drained apples in a greased baking dish. Cover apples with topping and press down firmly.
4. Bake 350°F for 30–40 minutes.

Note: Use reconstituted dehydrated apricots, peaches, or prunes in place of the dehydrated apples. Leave out shredded cheese if desired.

« APRICOT COBBLER »

Yield: 6 servings

3 ½ cups dehydrated apricots
3 ½ cups water
1 cup and 1 tablespoon sugar
pastry for 8-inch double crust

2 or 3 drops almond extract
1 tablespoon firm butter
¼ cup white corn syrup
2 tablespoons cream

1. Move oven rack to 5 inches above bottom of oven, then preheat oven to 450°F.
2. Soak apricots in water until reconstituted, then drain.
3. Roll ¾ of pastry out into a 10 × 14-inch rectangle. Fold in half then gently lift into 10 ½ × 6 ½ × 2-inch glass or aluminum baking pan (or approximately this size). Unfold the pastry carefully so as not to tear, fitting it into angles of pan. Dough will extend about 1 ½ inches over side of pan. Sprinkle bottom of dough with ¼ cup sugar.
4. Put drained reconstituted apricots in bottom of pan over top of sugar, spreading evenly. Sprinkle with ¾ cup sugar and almond extract, then dot with butter and drizzle with corn syrup.
5. Bring extending dough up over apricots. Cut small squares of dough out of corners so it will fold neatly. There should be about 7 × 4-inch rectangle of fruit uncovered. Roll out remaining pastry dough into a rectangle. Cut into ½-inch-wide strips. Place strips of right length crisscross over apricots. Cover strip ends with 4 strips.
6. Brush top with cream and sprinkle on remaining sugar.
7. Bake 17–20 minutes, then reduce heat to 375°F and bake 25–30 minutes longer or until well-browned and juice bubbles up between strips. Remove to cake rack to cool. Serve lukewarm.

« APRICOT FRITTERS »

1 cup dehydrated apricots
1 cup water
1 cup all-purpose flour
1 teaspoon baking powder
½ teaspoon salt

3 tablespoons sugar
1 egg
⅓ cup milk
1 teaspoon melted butter

1. Soak apricots in water for half an hour or until reconstituted, then drain. Cut apricots into bite-sized pieces.
2. Sift together flour, baking powder, salt, and sugar.
3. Beat egg, then add in milk and melted butter. Mix well. Add flour mixture and beat to a smooth batter.
4. Fold in reconstituted apricots.
5. In a 3-quart frying kettle, heat shortening to 350°F. No frying basket is needed for fritters.
6. Dip spoon into hot fat and quickly dip up a heaping teaspoon of batter, and with a second spoon quickly push it into the fat. Work quickly so 6 or 7 fritters can fry at the same time. Temperature drops quite fast but try to maintain it around 350°F throughout frying.
7. Turn fritters when brown on underside. It requires 4–5 minutes to fry fritters of this size to a golden brown and to cook all the way through. Lift out quickly with food fork or slotted spoon onto paper towels to drain.
8. Serve hot like pancakes with sugar or syrup, or serve sprinkled with powdered sugar for dessert.

« APRICOT WHIP »

Yield: 4–5 servings

¾ cup dehydrated apricots
¾ cup water
2 egg whites

2–3 drops almond extract
¼ cup sugar
1/16 teaspoon salt

1. Soak apricots in water until rehydrated. Drain, reserving 2 tablespoons of the liquid. Chop apricots finely.
2. Put the egg whites, reserved liquid, almond extract, sugar, and salt in top of double boiler.
3. Stir well. Place over gently boiling water and immediately start beating with a rotary or electric beater as in making 7-Minute Icing and continue beating about 7 minutes with rotary beater or 4 minutes with electric, or until meringue holds stiff pointed peaks.
4. Remove pan from boiling water. Lift out beater and clean off. Use rubber spatula to fold in fruit gradually until just distributed. Scoop whip gently into a serving dish or heap lightly into sherbets and serve immediately or place in refrigerator to chill.

« BANANA FRITTERS »

¾ cup dehydrated bananas
1 cup water
1 cup all-purpose flour
1 teaspoon baking powder
½ teaspoon salt

3 tablespoons sugar
1 egg
1/3 cup milk
1 teaspoon melted butter

1. Soak bananas in water for half hour or until reconstituted. Drain.
2. Sift together flour, baking powder, salt, and sugar.
3. Beat egg, then mix in milk and melted butter. Add dry ingredients and beat to a smooth batter. Fold in reconstituted bananas.
4. In a 3-quart frying kettle, heat shortening to 350°F. No frying basket is needed for fritters.
5. Dip spoon into hot fat and quickly dip up a heaping teaspoon of batter, and with a second spoon quickly push it into the fat. Work quickly so 6 or 7 fritters can fry at the same time. Temperature drops quite fast but try to maintain it around 350°F throughout frying.
6. Turn fritters when brown on underside. It requires 4–5 minutes to fry fritters of this size to a golden brown and to cook all the way through. Lift out quickly with food fork or slotted spoon onto paper towels to drain.
7. Serve hot like pancakes with sugar or syrup, or serve sprinkled with powdered sugar for dessert.

« CARROT PUDDING »

Yield: 6–8 servings

¼ cup dehydrated carrots
½ cup water
1 ¾ cups all-purpose flour
1 ½ teaspoons baking powder
½ teaspoon salt
¼ teaspoon baking soda

⅓ cup shortening
1 cup sugar
1 teaspoon lemon extract
1 egg, beaten
1 cup buttermilk

1. Preheat oven to 375°F. Grease a 9 × 9 × 2-inch pan with butter.
2. Soak carrots in water until reconstituted then cut into very small pieces.
3. Sift together flour, baking powder, salt, and baking soda.
4. Cream the shortening, then add the sugar, lemon extract, and egg.
5. Add to this, in turns, the buttermilk and the flour mixture. Beat smooth after each addition. When batter is mixed, sprinkle over and fold in the pieces of carrots, distributing them evenly.
6. Turn batter into prepared pan, spreading a little higher at edge of pan than in center. Bake 30–35 minutes or until pudding tests done. Remove to cake rack, cool to lukewarm.
7. Cut in serving portions, lift onto dessert plates, and serve with Nutmeg Pudding Sauce.

« NUTMEG PUDDING SAUCE »

Yield: 1 ⅓ cups

¾ cup granulated sugar
1 tablespoon plus 1 ½ teaspoons flour
¼ teaspoon salt
1 cup boiling water

1 tablespoon cider vinegar
1 ½ tablespoons brown sugar
2 tablespoons firm butter
Scant ½ teaspoon nutmeg

1. Blend in saucepan the sugar, flour, and salt. Gradually stir in boiling water, making sure the mixture stays smooth.
2. When all of the water has been added, pour in vinegar. Stir and cook over moderate direct heat until thick and clear, 4–5 minutes.
3. Remove from heat and stir in brown sugar, butter, and nutmeg. Serve warm or cold.

« BLACKSTONE WINTER FRUIT COMPOTE »

Yield: 7–8 servings

1 pound mixed dried fruit
3 cups water
¾ cup sugar

dash salt
¼ cup white corn syrup

1. Wash dried fruit quickly and thoroughly in cold water. Drain, then add washed fruit to water. Cover and heat to boiling, then reduce heat and simmer for 20 minutes.
2. In the last 5 minutes of cooking, add the sugar, salt, and corn syrup.
3. Keep covered while cooling, then chill. The fruit should be whole but tender and the syrup clear and thick.

« DRIED FRUIT COMPOTE »

Yield: 5–6 servings

½ cup dried apricots
½ cup seedless raisins
½ cup dried figs
½ cup dried prunes

½ cup pitted dates
⅓ cup lemon juice
¼ cup honey

1. Wash fruit quickly in cold water, then drain and pat dry with paper towels.
2. Put fruit through food processor, alternating the fruit as you chop them so they will be somewhat mixed, dropping them into a mixing bowl. Drizzle lemon juice and honey over fruit, mixing well.

3. Cover tightly and place in refrigerator for a day or so for fruits to soften and for flavors to blend. To serve, heap cold mixture lightly in sherbet glasses and pour cream around fruit heap, then top with a puff of whipped cream.

« LIME HONEY FRUIT COMPOTE »

Yield: 4 servings

½ teaspoon green lime rind
¼ cup lime juice (roughly 2 green limes)
4 medium-sized apples
   (cored but not peeled)
¼ cup honey

¼ cup seedless raisins
1 dozen moist medium-sized prunes
   (cut small)
1 dozen pitted dates
¼ cup pecans or walnuts

1. Mix lime rind and juice together, then grate apples into mixture. Add the honey, raisins, prunes, and dates to this and mix well. Cover, and chill 12–24 hours for flavors to blend.
2. Just before serving, stir in nuts.
3. Heap lightly into dishes and serve with cream.

Note: Mixed dried fruit may be used to make this dessert.

« CHERRY COBBLER »

Yield: 4–5 servings

3 ½ cups dehydrated pie cherries
3 ½ cups water
1 cup and 1 teaspoon sugar
½ and ¼ teaspoon salt
2 teaspoons cornstarch

1 ½ cups all-purpose flour
1 teaspoon baking powder
⅓ cup shortening
½ cup plus 1 ½ tablespoons milk

1. Soak cherries in water until reconstituted. Drain, reserving liquid.
2. Together in bowl, add 1 cup sugar, ½ teaspoon salt, and cornstarch.
3. Sift together the flour, 1 teaspoon sugar, ¼ teaspoon salt, and baking powder. Cut in the shortening with pastry blender until particles are size of rice. When all of the shortening has been cut in, add milk. Stir vigorously with a fork to mix.
4. Turn out ¾ of the dough onto a floured pastry cloth. Shape into a rectangle, then roll out to about 13 ½ × 12 inches. Fold dough in half and lift into baking dish, then carefully unfold and fit into angles of pan. There should be about an inch of dough extending over rim of dish.
5. Sprinkle ⅓ of the sugar mixture over bottom of dough; add reconstituted drained cherries, spreading evenly. Sprinkle on rest of sugar, then dot with butter. Fold

A cobbler made from dehydrated cherries.

extending dough up over fruit. This leaves a strip of cherries uncovered in center. Roll out rest of dough slightly larger than exposed cherries, and cut design in center for steam vents. Lay over cherries, overlapping other dough a little.

6. Bake for 15 minutes at 450°F and then reduce heat to 325°F and bake 10–15 minutes longer or until richly browned and cherries are tender. Cool on cake rack to lukewarm.

Note: If you find the cherries are too dry this way, add ½ cup of drained liquid to cherries as they are poured into the bottom of the pan.

« CHERRY MARSHMALLOW DESSERT »

Yield: 5–6 servings

2 cups dehydrated sour pie cherries	1 cup whipping cream
2 cups water	⅛ teaspoon salt
1 cup sugar	¼ teaspoon almond extract
32 marshmallows (½ pound)	1 tablespoon lemon juice

1. Soak cherries in water until reconstituted, then simmer until tender and add sugar. Mix thoroughly and cook 10 minutes more. Then cool, drain, and cut cherries into small pieces. Reserve liquid.
2. Put ½ cup drained cherry juice and marshmallows in top of double boiler. Place over boiling water until marshmallows are melted but still fluffy. Remove from heat

and stir in the finely chopped cherries. Add salt and almond extract. Mix well; chill thoroughly.

3. Whip the whipping cream until thick, then add in the lemon juice. Continue whipping until stiff.

4. Fold cherry mixture into whipped cream, pour into freezing tray of refrigerator, and freeze at lowest temperature until firm, stirring once or twice if cherries tend to sink to the bottom.

« CHERRY UPSIDE-DOWN PUDDING »

Yield: 7–8 servings

2 ½ cups dehydrated sour pie cherries
2 ½ cups water
1 ¾ cups sugar
1 ½ cups all-purpose flour
1 ½ teaspoons baking powder

¼ teaspoon salt
½ cup soft butter, margarine, or shortening
⅛ teaspoon almond extract
1 egg
1 cup milk

1. Soak cherries in water until reconstituted, then simmer until tender. Add in ¾ cup of sugar. Blend until sugar is dissolved, stirring occasionally. Remove from heat, but keep hot.

2. Sift together the flour, baking powder, and salt.

3. Cream the soft butter, margarine, or shortening, then gradually add in 1 cup sugar. Cream mixture well. Stir in almond extract, and then beat in egg until mixture is fluffy.

4. Alternately with flour mixture, add in the milk to the creamed mixture, beginning and ending with flour. Beat batter well after each addition.

5. Turn into greased 8 × 8 × 2-inch glass baking dish, spreading evenly. Gently pour hot cherries and juice over batter. Bake 35–40 minutes at 350°F oven, or until top springs back when lightly pressed with fingertips. Remove to cake rack; cool to lukewarm. Spoon warm pudding into dishes.

« PEACH COBBLER »

Yield: 6 servings

6 cups dehydrated peaches
6 cups water
1 cup plus 2 tablespoons sugar
⅛ teaspoon salt
1 ½ cups and 1 tablespoon flour
1 teaspoon baking powder

⅓ cup shortening
½ cup plus 1 ½ tablespoons milk
2 tablespoons fine dry white bread crumbs
2 tablespoons cream

1. Adjust rack to middle of oven and preheat to 450°F. Soak peaches in water until reconstituted, then drain.
2. Blend together 1 cup sugar and 1 tablespoon flour. Set sugar mixture aside. Sift together the 1 ½ cups flour, 2 tablespoons sugar, ⅛ teaspoon salt, and baking powder. Cut in the shortening with pastry blender until particles are the size of rice. When all of the shortening has been cut in, add milk. Stir vigorously with a fork to mix.
3. Turn out ¾ of the dough onto a floured pastry cloth. Shape into a rectangle, then roll out to about 14 ½ × 10 ½ inches. Fold dough in half and lift into baking dish, then carefully unfold and fit into angles of pan. There should be about 1 ½ inches of dough extending over rim of dish.
4. Sprinkle bread crumbs over bottom of a 10 ¼ × 6 ¼ × 2-inch glass or aluminum baking pan, then spread ¼ cup of the sugar mixture over the crumbs.
5. Spread drained peaches into pan, spreading evenly. Dot with butter and sprinkle with the rest of the sugar mixture. Fold extending dough neatly up over peaches; cut out a little square of dough at each corner to prevent the pastry from being too thick. Tuck in ends at the four corners neatly. There will be an area of about 2 × 6 inches of peaches in the center that will not be covered with pastry. Roll out rest of pastry into a rectangle about 3 × 7 inches. Trim off edges neatly and cut a long design down the center to cover peaches.
6. Brush entire top lightly but completely with cream, then sprinkle evenly with sugar, a teaspoon or so, for an interesting surface. Bake 15–17 minutes or until crust starts browning. Reduce heat to 325°F and bake 25 minutes, or until bottom and top crusts are a rich brown and juice starts bubbling up through the vents.
7. Remove to cake rack to cool. Serve lukewarm, plain or with cream.

« PEACH LAYER CRISP DESSERT »

Yield: 8 servings

2 cups dehydrated peaches	½ cup white sugar
4 cups hot water	2 tablespoons cornstarch
¼ cup butter or shortening	dash of salt
¼ cup brown sugar, packed	½ cup peach syrup
¼ cup sifted flour	½ cup milk
½ teaspoon salt	2 eggs
2 cups cornflakes or graham crackers	½ teaspoon vanilla

1. Simmer peaches in water until tender, then let cool. Drain peaches, reserving syrup.
2. Blend butter or shortening, brown sugar, flour, and salt until crumbly. Add cornflakes or graham crackers and mix lightly. Press half of the above mixture into bottom and on sides of greased 8-inch square pan.
3. Blend white sugar, cornstarch, and dash of salt, then add peach syrup and milk. Mix until smooth and cook, stirring frequently until thickened.

4. Beat eggs lightly. Stir small amount of hot mixture in with eggs and then combine eggs with remaining hot mixture and cook 2 minutes more, stirring constantly. Add peach slices and vanilla.
5. Pour over crumb mixture in pan. Sprinkle with remaining crumb mixture. Bake at 350°F for 30 minutes. Serve warm or cold.

« PRUNE MARSHMALLOW DESSERT »

Yield: 5 servings

½ cup dehydrated prunes
1 cup water
16 marshmallows (¼ pound)

1 cup whipping cream
2 tablespoons lemon juice

1. Soak prunes in water until reconstituted. Cook 10 minutes until prunes are softened. Drain off ¾ liquid, reserving it for later, and put the rest of the water and the prunes in a blender to make a puree.
2. Heat reserved liquid to boiling; remove from heat and add marshmallows. Beat with rotary beater until they are melted and mixture is smooth. Beat in prune puree and 2 tablespoons lemon juice and turn into freezing tray of refrigerator. Freeze about 1 hour, then remove to a chilled bowl and beat well. Whip and then fold in the whipping cream.
3. Return immediately to chilled tray and continue freezing until firm.

« BAKED PRUNE PUDDING »

Yield: 4 servings

1 cup dehydrated prunes or plums
1 cup hot water
¼ teaspoon grated lemon rind
¼ cup coarsely broken walnuts
½ cup graham cracker crumbs
   (eight 2-inch squares)

⅓ cup sugar
¾ teaspoon baking powder
¼ teaspoon salt
½ cup room temperature milk
1 teaspoon vanilla
1 tablespoon melted butter

1. Soak prunes or plums in hot water until reconstituted. Cook until tender. Drain and cut prunes or plums into small pieces. Add in the lemon rind, walnuts, and graham cracker crumbs.
2. In a 2 quart mixing bowl, mix sugar, baking powder, salt, milk, vanilla, and melted butter. Fold in prune mixture thoroughly. Turn into buttered 8 ½ × 4 ½ × 1 ¾-inch glass loaf pan or a 4-cup casserole dish.
3. Bake uncovered at 375°F for 35 minutes or until pudding has a thin brown crust over top and around sides. Serve warm with cream or Soft Hard Sauce.

« PRUNE WHIP »

Yield: 4–5 servings

1 cup dehydrated prunes or plums
1 cup hot water
1 cup pitted, stewed prunes or plums,
  chopped fine
2 egg whites

2 teaspoons lemon juice and
⅛ teaspoon grated lemon rind
¼ cup sugar
¹⁄₁₆ teaspoon salt

1. Soak prunes or plums in hot water until reconstituted. Cook until tender. Drain, reserving 2 tablespoons of the juice, and cut prunes or plums into small pieces.
2. In the top of a double boiler, add the egg whites, reserved juice, lemon juice, lemon rind, sugar, and salt. Stir well.
3. Place over gently boiling water and immediately start beating with a rotary or electric beater as in making a 7-Minute Icing, and continue beating about 7 minutes with rotary beater or 4 minutes with electric beater, or until meringue holds stiff pointed peaks. Remove pan from boiling water.
4. Lift out beater and clean off. Now, using rubber scraper, fold in fruit gradually until just distributed. Turn whip gently into a serving dish, heap lightly into sherbets and serve immediately, or place in refrigerator to chill.

« RHUBARB COBBLER »

Yield: 6–8 servings

2 cups dehydrated rhubarb
4 cups water

1 cup sugar (or to taste)
1 tablespoon butter

1. Cook rhubarb in water on medium heat until tender and reconstituted. Add sugar and butter to cooked mixture.
2. Put rhubarb in bottom of a deep dish. Pour Pudding Batter over it.
3. Bake in 350°F oven for 20–30 minutes until batter is done. Serve hot with cream.

Note: Dehydrated strawberries can be used in place of the rhubarb or 1 cup dehydrated rhubarb and 1 cup dehydrated strawberries will make a delicious cobbler.

« PUDDING BATTER »

3 tablespoons butter
½ cup sugar
1 egg, well beaten

½ cup milk
1 cup flour
1 teaspoon vanilla

1. Cream together butter and sugar, then add the egg and mix well. Add milk and vanilla, mixing thoroughly. Sift flour and add it to the creamed mixture.
2. Beat smooth, then pour over rhubarb.

« RHUBARB CRUMBLE »

2 cups dehydrated rhubarb
4 cups and 3 tablespoons warm water
⅔ cup white sugar
⅓ cup flour
¼ teaspoon salt

½ teaspoon cinnamon
1 cup brown sugar
¾ cup flour
¾ cup margarine or butter
½ teaspoon salt

1. Mix rhubarb in 4 cups of water and let sit 30 minutes. Drain, then add white sugar, flour, and salt. Place in buttered baking dish. Sprinkle with cinnamon.
2. Mix together brown sugar, flour, margarine or butter, and salt and pour over rhubarb mixture as a topping. Sprinkle with 3 tablespoons of water.
3. Bake at 350°F for about 40 minutes. Serve warm or cold, plain or with sour cream, whipped cream, ice cream, or cheese.

« RHUBARB TAPIOCA »

Yield: 6–8 servings

1 ½ cups dehydrated rhubarb
3 cups plus 2 ½ cups warm water
1 ¼ cups sugar
¼ cup minute tapioca

½ teaspoon salt
3 drops red color, if desired
1 cup crushed pineapple

1. Soak rhubarb in 3 cups of water and let sit 30 minutes until reconstituted, then drain. Combine rhubarb with sugar, tapioca, salt, red food coloring, and 2 ½ cups of water.
2. Cook over medium heat, stirring constantly until full boil, stirring occasionally to avoid bubbling over. Cool slightly and add crushed pineapple. Chill and serve.

CHAPTER XV
« DRESSING RECIPES »

« APPLE DRESSING »

2 cups dehydrated apples
2 cups water
1 medium onion, peeled and chopped

2 tablespoons sugar
2 cups soft bread crumbs

1. Soak apples in water until reconstituted and a bit crisp, then drain.
2. Sauté onion in a small amount of oil or shortening. When onion is sautéed, add in drained apples, sugar, and bread crumbs. Mix ingredients well.
3. Heap dressing on top of browned meat, which should be well above surface of the liquid in the pan or the dressing will become soggy. Cover the meat and bake in moderately low oven until the meat is very tender.
4. Remove, cover, and continue to cook about 15 minutes to brown dressing slightly.

Note: This is excellent when used with veal; try with other meats to suit your own taste.

« CELERY STUFFING »

Yield: enough for a 4-pound chicken

1 tablespoon dehydrated onion
¾ cup dehydrated celery
1 ½ cups water
¾ pound loaf stale white bread
3 tablespoons butter

½ teaspoon poultry seasoning
1 teaspoon salt
⅛ teaspoon pepper
½ cup broth from cooking giblets or ½ cup milk

1. Soak onions and celery in water until reconstituted. Drain.
2. Tear bread into small pieces until there are about 6 cups of coarse crumbs.
3. Melt butter in saucepan and add in onion and celery. Cook, stirring frequently until mixture is soft and yellow.

4. Add bread crumbs, poultry seasonings, salt, and pepper. Toss together until well mixed. Cool, then add in milk or broth.
5. Mix lightly with a fork and stuff lightly into the dressed chicken.

« CORNBREAD DRESSING »

Yield: makes enough for 12-pound turkey

½ cup dehydrated celery
¼ cup dehydrated onion
¼ cup dehydrated green pepper
2 cups water
5–6 cups corn bread (pg. 69–70)
½ cup butter or margarine
½ cup shortening

1 cup chopped nuts (optional)
2 teaspoons salt
½ teaspoon pepper
1 ½ teaspoons poultry seasoning
2 eggs, beaten
1–1 ½ cups broth

1. Soak celery, onion, and green peppers in water until reconstituted, then drain.
2. Crumble the corn bread into crumbs. Cut butter or margarine into small pieces and then add to crumbs.
3. Heat shortening in skillet and add the nuts and drained vegetables. Sauté slowly for 10 minutes, then remove from heat.
4. To corn bread, add sautéed mixture, salt, pepper, and poultry seasoning, mixing thoroughly. When mixed, add in eggs. Mix well.
5. Sprinkle broth over corn bread and vegetable mixture. Stir lightly until dressing is of desired moistness.
6. Stuff lightly into breast region and body cavity of the bird.

CHAPTER XVI
« FRUIT RECIPES »

« PUREE OF ANY DRIED FRUIT »

Yield: 2 ½ cups
Excellent for baby food or older kids making fruit whips.

1 pound moist dried fruit	⅔ to 1 ⅓ cups sugar depending
1 ½ cups water	on tartness of fruit

1. Wash fruit quickly but thoroughly in cold water, lifting out into a 3-quart saucepan. Add water, which should come 1 inch above top of fruit. Cover and let soak 1–3 hours. Cook in same water in which fruit soaked. Now heat to boiling over moderate heat, then reduce heat and simmer until tender, 15–20 minutes. Stir in sugar in last 5 minutes of cooking, and cook until sugar dissolves. Remove from heat and cool to room temperature, then drain, saving juice.
2. Turn fruit into a sieve or food mill and rub through thoroughly to obtain all puree. Or, put fruit into a bowl and use kitchen scissors or biscuit cutter to chop the fruit finely (or use a commercially bought unit for making puree). If puree is thicker than desired, add enough of the drained-off juice to give desired consistency. A stiff puree is preferred for cake fillings and a medium one for fruit whip.
3. To store, pour puree into a sterilized jar with tight-fitting cover and keep in refrigerator.

Note: Use leftover juice over fruit cups or for beverage.

« DRIED APRICOT PUREE »

Yield: 2 cups
Excellent for making ice cream or fruit whip to serve to babies or older kids.

Stew apricots as described in Stewed Dried Apricots. Add sugar or leave unsweetened, depending on how puree is to be used.

Turn apricots into a sieve or food mill placed over a bowl. Let stand until syrup drains off. Pour syrup into a container and save for making fruit cocktails or for a beverage.

Now rub fruit through sieve or food mill to obtain all the puree. There should be 2 cups stiff puree. If a thinner puree is desired, thin it with some of the juice drained off.

« STEWED DRIED FRUIT (ANY KIND) »

Peaches, pears, and figs may be cooked in the following way to make a good simple dessert.

Prepare exactly like Stewed Dried Apricots, except add sugar to suit taste, allowing ⅓ to ⅔ cup sugar per each pound of fruit. Amount depends on tartness of fruit and personal taste. Some prefer to add no sugar at all.

« STEWED DRIED APPLES »

Yield: 6 cups thick sauce

1 pound dried apples   5 cups cold water
½ cup sugar

1. Place apples in a 4-quart saucepan, add cold water, cover, and soak 3 to 4 hours (although this may not be necessary). Heat to boiling over moderate heat, then reduce heat, cover, and simmer 15 to 20 minutes or until soft, but not mushy.
2. Stir in sugar and simmer 5 minutes longer. Remove from heat. Cool to lukewarm or chill.

« STEWED DRIED APRICOTS »

1 pound dried apricots   6 cups cold water
1 cup sugar   dash of salt (optional)

For attractive, appetizing results, use clean, brightly-colored fruit.

1. Wash quickly but thoroughly in cold water. Put fruit in a 3-quart saucepan, add water, cover, and let stand 1–2 hours. Then place over moderate heat until fruit begins to boil vigorously. Reduce heat immediately to a simmer and cook 12–15 minutes longer or until just soft.
2. Add sugar and salt and let simmer another 5 minutes. Remove from heat to cool to lukewarm, or chill to serve plain or with cream.

White raisins are obtained by dehydrating Thompson Seedless grapes.
Dark raisins are obtained by dehydrating Bing Cherries.
Raisins can be used in many different recipes:

tarts	carrot spread
pudding	bread
crumb pudding	cookies
pie	cakes
sauces	salads
stews	

Use your imagination and thoroughly enjoy the delicious flavor of the raisin!

CHAPTER XVII
« ICE CREAM RECIPES »

« APRICOT ICE CREAM »

Yield: 5 generous servings

1 cup dehydrated apricots
1 ¼ cups water
½ cup sugar
2 egg whites, stiffly beaten

⅔ cup whipping cream or evaporated
    milk
⅛ teaspoon almond extract

1. Soak apricots in 1 cup water until reconstituted, then cook in same water for 5–10 minutes or until soft. Put apricots and water in a blender and make a puree. There should be 1 cup of pulp and liquid. If not, add water to make 1 cup. Cool, then chill about 15 minutes.
2. Boil together the sugar and ¼ cup water until syrup forms, then pour hot syrup over stiffly beaten egg whites and beat together until smooth and thick. Chill for 15 minutes.
3. Put whipping cream or evaporated milk in a bowl, keeping it chilled by surrounding the bowl with chipped ice, and whip until very thick. Add the almond extract and continue whipping until stiff.
4. Fold in chilled apricot puree; then fold in the egg white mixture lightly but thoroughly. Place in the freezer and keep there until firm.

« BANANA ICE CREAM »

Yield: 1 ¼ quarts

2 cups dehydrated bananas
2 cups water
½ cup plus 2 tablespoons sugar
1 tablespoon flour
⅛ teaspoon salt

1 cup milk
1 cup half-and-half
½ cup whipping cream
1 tablespoon lemon juice

1. Soak bananas in water until reconstituted, approximately half an hour. Then put water and bananas into blender to make a puree.
2. In top part of double boiler, blend together ½ cup sugar, flour, and salt. Stir in milk and half-and-half until smooth.
3. Place over boiling water and cook and stir until milk is steaming hot and the flour is cooked, about 10 minutes. Remove from heat and set in ice water, stirring occasionally until custard is cold.
4. Stir in banana puree, then blend in whipping cream, lemon juice, and remaining sugar. Blend thoroughly until mixed and place at once into freezer and freeze until firm.

« PEACH ICE CREAM »

Yield: 6 servings

2 ¼ cups dehydrated peaches
2 ¼ cups water
1 ¼ cups whipping cream
2 teaspoons lemon juice

dash of salt
1 cup sugar
⅛ teaspoon almond extract

1. Soak peaches in water until reconstituted, then blend reconstituted peaches and liquid until pureed.
2. Thoroughly chill and whip whipping cream in a chilled bowl until thick. Add in the lemon juice and salt, then continue beating until very stiff. Beat in peach puree, sugar, and almond extract.
3. Place in the freezer for about 2 hours.

Peach ice cream is a tasty desert that is easy to make at home.

CHAPTER XVIII
« MEAT RECIPES »

« CHICKEN A LA KING »

Yield: 5 servings

1 ½ cups cooked dehydrated chicken chunks
2 tablespoons dehydrated green pepper
2 ¼ cups water
2 tablespoons butter or margarine
¼ pound fresh mushrooms, sliced
¼ cup flour
1 ⅓ cups cream or evaporated milk
½ pimiento, cut in strips

1. Soak chicken in 2 cups of water until reconstituted. Soak green peppers in ¼ cup of water until reconstituted. Drain both, reserving 1 ⅓ cups rich chicken broth from reconstituting chicken. Set aside.
2. Melt the butter or margarine in top of double boiler over direct heat, then add the reconstituted green peppers and mushrooms. Cover and simmer for 5 minutes, then remove peppers and mushrooms.
3. Blend the flour into fat, then add in the cream or evaporated milk, chicken broth, and salt and pepper to taste.
4. Cook with constant stirring over direct heat, until sauce boils and thickens. When thickened, add reconstituted chicken, green peppers, pimiento, and mushrooms. Place over boiling water, cover, and cook until chicken is heated through.
5. Serve hot over toast, biscuits, crisp noodles, or boiled rice.

« CHICKEN 'N' RICE »

Yield: 6 servings

5 cups dehydrated chicken chunks
¼ cup dehydrated celery stalk and leaves
½ cup dehydrated carrots
¼ cup dehydrated onions
1 teaspoon dehydrated green pepper
7 cups water
1 quart tomato juice
1 cup raw rice, not rinsed
1 teaspoon sugar
2 teaspoons salt

1. Soak chicken in 5 cups of water until reconstituted. Drain, reserving 2 cups of liquid. Soak celery and leaves, carrots, onions, and green peppers in 2 cups of water until reconstituted.
2. Put drained chicken in a heavy skillet or Dutch oven that has a tight fitting cover and add in tomato juice and reserved liquid. Simmer 15 minutes, then add in drained vegetables, rice, sugar, and salt.
3. Cook approximately 30 minutes until rice is tender. This will require frequent but careful stirring. This mixture becomes thick and must be stirred gently; careless stirring will cause the rice to become mushy.

Chicken 'N' Rice.

« CHICKEN CURRY »

Yield: 4 servings

1 ½ cups cooked dehydrated chicken
   chunks
3 ½ cups water
¼ cup dehydrated onions
3 tablespoons butter or margarine

½ cup flour
1 teaspoon lemon juice
1 teaspoon salt
2 teaspoons curry powder

1. Soak chicken in 3 cups of water until reconstituted. Drain, reserving liquid. Soak onions in ½ cup of water until reconstituted. Drain.
2. Melt butter or margarine in saucepan, then add in drained onions. Sauté until cooked.

3. In another saucepan over direct heat, brown flour. Stir constantly until it has a very light tan color, then blend flour into onions. Slowly add reserved liquid and mix constantly to keep smooth.

4. After mixture has thickened, add lemon juice and simmer 5 minutes, stirring occasionally. Add drained chicken.

5. Heat thoroughly, stirring occasionally. Serve over hot fluffy rice with freshly grated coconut, chutney, chopped salted peanuts, or chopped parsley.

« CHICKEN LOAF WITH MUSHROOM SAUCE »

Yield: 4–5 servings

1 ½ cups cooked dehydrated chicken
3 cups water
⅓ cup dehydrated celery
¼ cup dehydrated onion
½ cup water
3 tablespoons butter or margarine

6 slices day-old bread
⅛ teaspoon pepper
½ teaspoon poultry seasoning
1 teaspoon salt
1 egg, beaten

1. Soak chicken in 3 cups of water until reconstituted, then drain, reserving ½ cup of liquid. Soak celery and onion in ½ cup of water until reconstituted; drain.

2. In skillet, melt butter or margarine, then add in drained onions and celery. Sauté 4–5 minutes or until soft, stirring occasionally.

3. Tear bread into bite-size pieces and add to drained chicken. Sprinkle pepper, poultry seasoning, and salt over bread. Add beaten egg and stir in chicken broth. Mix with 2 forks very thoroughly; place mixture into greased 8 ¾ × 4 ¾ × 2 ½-inch pan, but don't pack down too firmly.

4. Bake 30–35 minutes at 350°F until nicely browned on top. Unmold onto hot platter. Serve with Mushroom Sauce.

« MUSHROOM SAUCE »

4 teaspoons margarine or butter
¾ cup sliced mushrooms
2 tablespoons flour

1 ½ cups milk
½ teaspoon salt
⅛ teaspoon pepper

1. Melt butter or margarine in saucepan, then add in mushrooms. Toss for 1 minute. Cover and cook 2–3 minutes until mushrooms are juicy. Uncover, push mushrooms to one side.
2. Stir in flour and gradually add in milk. Cook and stir until thickened and smooth. Stir in salt and pepper and serve hot over Chicken Loaf.

« CHICKEN NOODLES »

Yield: 4–5 servings

1 cup cooked dehydrated chicken
1 cup water
5 ounces narrow noodles
¾ teaspoon salt
4 ½ tablespoons butter or margarine
¾ cup sliced mushrooms
2 ½ tablespoons flour

¾ cup milk
8 ripe olives, cut in half
1 tablespoon pimiento, cut in ½ inch pieces
½ cup freshly grated Parmesan or aged American cheese

1. Soak chicken in water until reconstituted, then drain. Reserve ¾ cup liquid.
2. Drop noodles into 1 quart of boiling water and add salt. Cook until just tender, 6–8 minutes; drain noodles and turn into a buttered 9-inch pie plate.
3. Melt butter or margarine in saucepan, then add in mushrooms. Sauté 2–3 minutes or until mushrooms are juicy. Push mushrooms to side, remove pan from heat.
4. Blend in flour and stir until smooth. Slowly stir in milk and reserved liquid. Stir to keep smooth; place over moderate heat and cook, stirring, until mixture boils and thickens.
5. Add drained chicken, olives, and pimiento. Reheat mixture to boiling, remove from heat, and pour over noodles. Sprinkle cheese uniformly over top. Broil with surface 3 inches below source of heat to a tempting brown, about 6–8 minutes.

« CHICKEN PIE »

Yield: 5 servings

2 cups cooked dehydrated chicken
  chunks
3 cups water
⅓ cup dehydrated peas
⅓ cup dehydrated celery
½ cup cold broth
⅓ cup flour

1 teaspoon salt
1 cup flour
1 ½ teaspoons baking powder
¼ teaspoon salt
3 tablespoons butter or margarine
⅓ cup milk

1. Soak chicken in 2 cups of water until reconstituted. Drain, reserving 2 cups liquid. Place ½ cup of broth in refrigerator to chill. Soak peas and celery in 1 cup of water until reconstituted. Cover peas and celery and cook until tender over medium heat.
2. Make a paste by blending ½ cup of chilled, reserved liquid and flour until smooth. Add paste to 1 ½ cups hot chicken broth and heat to boiling. Cook over direct heat, stirring constantly until sauce boils and thickens. Combine with drained chicken, peas, and celery. Pour into a 6-cup buttered casserole.

3. Sift together flour, baking powder, and salt, then cut in butter or margarine with a pastry blender or 2 knives. When all of the butter or margarine has been cut in, quickly add milk. Stir quickly with a fork until dough just stiffens.
4. Turn dough out onto floured board, knead 8 times, and roll or pat out to make a circular sheet about 8 ½ inches in diameter or to fit top of casserole, and about ¼ inch thick. Make several cuts for a design near the center to allow steam to escape, and place on top of hot filling in casserole. Crimp edge of dough, pressing it firmly against edge of casserole.
5. Bake at 425°F for about 20 minutes, or until nicely browned with the filling boiling hot all the way through.

« BEEF JERKY »

Yield: Start with 2 pounds meat, bone, and fat; end with ½ pound jerky steak

1 tablespoon liquid smoke
1 package meat marinade
1 teaspoon salt (or less if you don't want it tasting too salty)
½–¾ cup water

1. Completely trim fat off meat. Using flank steak, sirloin tip, or round steak, cut fairly thick pieces, roughly ½–¾ inches thick. Cut strips ½ inches wide.
2. Mix together liquid smoke, marinade, and salt to make sauce. Put the sauce in a long shallow pan and add water. Let stand 30–60 minutes.
3. Put strips of meat in and marinade for 30 minutes. Fork out strips, drain, and lay on trays of dehydrator. Dehydrate for approximately 10 hours or until completely dry.

« IRISH STEW »

Yield: 5 servings

3 cups cooked dehydrated beef chunks	7 cups water
¼ cup dehydrated onion	3 beef bouillon cubes
3 cups dehydrated potatoes	2 teaspoons salt
1 ½ cups dehydrated carrots	dash of pepper

1. Soak beef in 3 cups of water until meat is reconstituted, then drain. Soak vegetables in 4 cups of water until reconstituted, then cook vegetables in covered saucepan until tender. Add in beef, bouillon cubes, salt, and pepper and stir.
2. Simmer until flavoring is evenly distributed. Serve hot.

Yield: 5 generous servings

3 cups cooked dehydrated beef
3 ¼ cups water
2 tablespoons dehydrated onion
2 cups cold cooked cereal
1 teaspoon salt
¼ teaspoon pepper

½ teaspoon celery salt
1 egg or 2 yolks, unbeaten
3 ½ cups sauerkraut and juice
⅓ cup brown sugar, firmly packed
2 tablespoons vinegar

1. Soak beef in 3 cups of water until reconstituted. Drain water off reconstituted beef; grind beef in food grinder. Reserve ¼ cup of liquid to be used later. Soak onion in ¼ cup of water until reconstituted, then drain.
2. Combine ground beef, cereal, onions, salt, pepper, celery salt, and egg. Blend thoroughly, shape into small balls, and brown slowly on all sides in a skillet in drippings.
3. Pour sauerkraut and juice over meat and mix, then add brown sugar, reserved liquid, and vinegar.
4. Cover and simmer about 20 minutes, or until meat balls are done through, and onion and egg mixture has cooked.

Old-fashioned hash.

« OLD-FASHIONED HASH »

Yield: 3–4 servings

1 ½ cups cooked dehydrated beef chunks
2 cups dehydrated potatoes
¼ cup dehydrated onion
3 ¾ cups water

1 ¼ teaspoons salt
⅛ teaspoon pepper
2 ½ tablespoons butter or margarine

1. Soak beef in 1 ½ cups of water until reconstituted, then drain. Soak onion in ½ cup of water until reconstituted. Drain and reserve liquid. Soak potatoes in 2 cups of water until reconstituted, then cover potatoes and cook over moderate heat until tender. Drain off water, reserving it for later, and chill potatoes. When chilled, cut into ¼-inch cubes.
2. Put beef, chopped potatoes, onions, salt, and pepper in bowl. Toss lightly with fork until mixed well.
3. Melt butter or margarine in skillet and add in 1 ¼ cups of reserved liquid. Heat to boiling, then add in meat mixture. Stir gently, then cover and cook over medium heat until meat has browned on one side, about 15 minutes. Turn carefully with spatula, and, if necessary, add a little more butter or margarine. Cover and brown mixture, but do not cook hash too dry. Total cooking time is 20–25 minutes.
4. Serve with chili sauce.

« BEEF PINWHEELS WITH MUSHROOM SAUCE »

Yield: 4–6 servings

2 cups cooked dehydrated beef chunks
¼ cup dehydrated onion
2 ½ cups water
4 tablespoons butter or margarine
½ cup gravy or 1 beef bouillon cube mixed in ½ cup hot water
1 teaspoon prepared horseradish
¼ teaspoon salt

2 cups Medium White Sauce (pg. 132)
½ pound mushrooms, cleaned and chopped
¼ cup finely chopped parsley or 2 tablespoons dehydrated parsley
1 batch of standard baking powder biscuit dough using 2 cups flour

1. Soak beef in 2 cups of water until reconstituted, then grind drained beef in a food mill. Soak onion in ½ cup of water until reconstituted, then drain.
2. Melt 2 tablespoons of butter or margarine in skillet and add in the drained onions. Sauté onions until slightly transparent, about 5 minutes. Add the ground beef, ½ cup of gravy or reconstituted bouillon cube, horseradish, and ¼ cup Medium White Sauce to onions. Let stand to cool.
3. Roll biscuit dough into 9 × 12-inch rectangle. Spread with meat mixture, then roll as for jelly roll. Seal edges and cut into 8 crosswise slices. Place on greased baking sheet, cut side down.

4. Bake at 425°F for 25–30 minutes. Cover pinwheels for the first 15 minutes with parchment paper to prevent drying out.
5. Melt the remaining butter or margarine in saucepan, then add and sauté the mushrooms. When mushrooms have sautéed, add in salt and remaining White Sauce. Heat mixture until boiling, then add in parsley. Serve hot over baked pinwheels.

Note: Ground reconstituted chicken chunks can be substituted for beef.

« BEEF OR CHICKEN TURNOVERS »

Yield: 5 servings

1 cup cooked dehydrated beef or chicken chunks	2 tablespoons butter
1 ¼ cups water	2 tablespoons flour
½ teaspoon dehydrated onion	1 beef or chicken bouillon cube
1 tablespoon dehydrated celery	1 batch of standard baking powder biscuit dough using 2 cups flour

1. Soak beef or chicken in 1 cup of water until reconstituted; drain, reserving ⅔ cup of liquid. Soak onion and celery in ¼ cup of water until reconstituted, then drain. Boil reserved liquid and mix in bouillon cube.
2. Melt butter in saucepan and sauté the drained meat. Blend in the flour until smooth, then gradually add in the reserved liquid. Stir constantly over medium heat until smooth and thickened. Add in drained onion and celery, then add salt and pepper to taste. Stir to blend and cool slightly.
3. Prepare recipe baking powder biscuit dough according to directions. Turn out on floured board and roll or pat out into a 6 × 15-inch rectangle ⅛ inch thick. Cut into 5 3 × 6-inch pieces. Heap ⅕ of the cooked meat mixture onto half of each piece of dough. Moisten edges and fold other half over meat. Press edges together with tines of fork to seal. Cut design in top of turnovers for steam vents.
4. Bake on a greased baking sheet at 425°F for 15–20 minutes or until crust is well browned. Serve at once with creamed mushrooms, peas, or other creamed vegetables.

CHAPTER XIX
« PIE RECIPES »

« APPLE PIE »

Yield: 5–6 servings

4 cups dehydrated apples
4 cups water
1 tablespoon flour
dash of salt
¾ cup sugar

1 tablespoon butter
1 tablespoon lemon juice, optional
¼ teaspoon cinnamon, optional
pastry crust

1. Soak apples in water until reconstituted; drain.
2. Bake a pastry for a 9-inch double crust. Roll out ½ of it to line 9-inch pie pan, fitting well into angles; trim dough to be even with pan rim. Roll out remaining pastry for

top crust. Cut design in center for wide-open steam vents. Cover pastry with waxed paper while preparing filling so that it won't dry out.

3. Blend together flour, salt, and sugar and sprinkle ¼ of mixture over bottom of pastry-lined pan. Stir rest of mixture lightly through drained apples and place them into pan, arranging slices to fit shell compactly. Fruit should be slightly rounded up in center. Dot with butter and sprinkle with lemon juice and cinnamon.

4. Moisten edge of lower pastry, then lay the top crust down on top, pressing down gently around the edge to seal the crust. Trim off pastry with scissors ½ inch beyond rim. Turn overhang under lower pastry so fold is even with pan rim. Again press down gently all around edge, and crimp with tines of fork or flute with fingers.

5. Bake 15 minutes, at 450°F, then reduce heat to 325°F and bake 35 minutes longer or until apples are tender and juice bubbles out of vents. Remove to cake rack to cool 2–3 hours. Serve lukewarm, plain, with cheese, or with ice cream.

« APRICOT PIE WITH LATTICE TOP »

Yield: 6–7 servings

1 ½ cups dehydrated apricots	½ cup sugar
1 ½ cups water	1 ½ tablespoons cornstarch
½ cup sugar	⅛ teaspoon salt
pastry crust	1 tablespoon butter

1. Preheat oven to 425°F.

2. Soak apricots in water until reconstituted, then add sugar. Place over heat, cover, and boil gently about 20 minutes or until fruit is tender. Quickly drain off juice, adding enough water to make 1 cup.

3. Make pastry for 8-inch double crust. Roll out a scant ⅔ of it and line a 9-inch pie pan, fitting well into angles. Trim off to be even with rim of pan. Roll out rest of pastry and cut into 18 strips ⅜ to ½ inch wide for lattice top. Set aside 2 longest strips to finish edge.

4. Blend together sugar, cornstarch, and salt. Sprinkle 2 tablespoons of the mixture over bottom of pastry-lined pan. Stir remainder of mixture gently into apricots and place into lined pan. Dot with butter.

5. Moisten edge of lower pastry. Lay 8 strips across top each way to form pastry top. Trim strips to be even with rim and again moisten edge. Lay the 2 longest strips around rim of pie and crimp with tines of fork to finish edge.

6. Bake about 30 minutes, or until crust is nicely browned and juice bubbles up through lattice. Remove to cake rack to cool 2–3 hours before cutting.

Cherry pie with lattice top.

« CHERRY PIE WITH LATTICE TOP »

Yield: 6 servings

2 cups dehydrated pie cherries	3 tablespoons cornstarch
4 cups water	3–4 drops of red food coloring (optional)
1 cup sugar (or to your taste)	pastry crust

1. Soak cherries in water until reconstituted, then cook over medium heat until fruit is tender. Let cool. Add sugar and cornstarch, stirring thoroughly and cook until thickened. Add food coloring.
2. Make pastry. Roll out a scant ⅔ of the pastry and line a 9-inch pie pan, fitting well into angles. Roll out remaining pastry into an oval and cut into 18 strips 3/8 to ½-inch wide for lattice top. Save the 2 longest strips to finish edge. Place cooked and thickened cherries into lined pan, spreading evenly. Trim pastry to be even with pan rim. Moisten edge. Lay 8 pastry strips each way across pie without interlacing to form lattice; press ends of strips against edge of lower crust. Now trim off strips to be even with rim. Again moisten edge slightly, lay the 2 long strips around edge, joining neatly, and crimp with tines of fork.

3. Bake about 30 minutes at 425°F or until crust is nicely browned and juice bubbles up through lattice. Remove to cake rack to cool 2–3 hours before cutting.

Note: A solid pie crust top can also be used.

« PEACH CRUMBLE PIE »

Yield: 6 servings

3 cups dehydrated peaches
3 cups water
¾ cup all-purpose flour

⅓ cup moist light brown sugar
⅓ cup firm butter or margarine
pastry crust

1. Preheat oven to 425°F and adjust rack until it is 5–6 inches from bottom.
2. Soak peaches in water until reconstituted; drain.
3. Blend together flour and sugar, then cut in the butter or margarine with pastry blender or 2 knives until particles are the size of peas. Chill until needed.
4. Make a pastry for 9-inch single crust. Roll out and line 9-inch pie pan, fitting well into angles. Let rest 5 minutes, then with scissors trim off ½ inch beyond pan rim. Fold overhang under so fold is even with pan rim. Flute edge with fingers or crimp with tines of fork.
5. Bake for 15 minutes, then reduce heat to 350°F and bake 20 minutes longer. Remove to cake rack and cool 2–3 hours. Serve lukewarm or cold.

« RHUBARB PIE »

Yield: 6 servings

2 ½ cups dehydrated rhubarb
2 ½ cups water
1–1 ¼ cups sugar

1–2 tablespoons flour
⅛ teaspoon salt

1. Soak rhubarb in water until reconstituted; drain.
2. Mix together sugar, flour, and salt. Spread ⅓ of this mixture over bottom of pastry-lined pan and place half of rhubarb over it; spread level and sprinkle with half of the remaining sugar mixture. Add rest of rhubarb, level, and sprinkle with rest of sugar mixture. Dot mixture with 1 tablespoon butter.
3. Trim pastry to be even with rim of pan; moisten edge with water. Lay on top pastry, pressing gently at rim to seal. Trim off top pastry with scissors, ½ inch beyond rim of pan; turn overhang under edge of lower pastry so fold is even with rim of pan. Again press gently to seal, then crimp with tines of fork or make shallow fluting with fingers.
4. Bake about 30 minutes at 425°F or until crust is nicely browned and juice bubbles up through vents. Remove to cake rack to cool 2–3 hours before cutting.

CHAPTER XX
« SAUCE AND TOPPING RECIPES »

« APRICOT GLAZE FOR FRUIT CAKE »

Yield: enough to double coat a 12–15 pound cake

½ cup dehydrated apricots
1 ½ cups water

1 cup white corn syrup

1. Soak apricots in water until reconstituted, then cook until tender, about 15 minutes.
2. Drain off juice through a sieve or food mill and rub only half the apricots through the sieve (or put half the apricots into a blender to make a puree). Use unsieved fruit as sauce. Measure juice and pureed fruit—there should be ½ cup.
3. Add 1 cup white corn syrup and boil rapidly 2–3 minutes or until mixture is clear. Remove from heat.
4. Apply immediately to fruit cake with a pastry brush. If desired, apply decorations after first coat of glaze, then add a second coat over decorations after first coat is set. Reheat glaze to boiling each time it is used.
5. Allow glaze to dry thoroughly before wrapping or storing cakes.

« CARROT SAUCE »

Yield: 2 cups

½ cup dehydrated carrots
1 cup water
1 tablespoon butter or margarine

1 tablespoon flour
1 bouillon cube
½ cup ketchup

1. Soak carrots in 1 cup of water until reconstituted, then drain off water, reserving it for later, and cut carrots into slivers.
2. Melt butter or margarine in saucepan and add in flour. Gradually add in reserved liquid. Cook over low heat until mixture is smooth and thickened, stirring constantly. Heat to boiling.

3. Add slivered carrots and cook for 5 minutes, stirring occasionally. The carrots will retain their crispness; if softer consistency is preferred, increase cooking time. Add in ketchup and stir thoroughly until blended. Serve with meat loaf, pea loaf, or pan-fried liver.

« CELERY SAUCE »

Yield: 2 ½ cups

⅓ cup dehydrated celery
⅔ cup water
¼ cup butter or margarine

¼ cup flour
2 cups milk

1. Soak celery in water until reconstituted; drain.
2. Melt butter or margarine in saucepan and add in drained celery. Simmer over low heat, stirring occasionally for 5 minutes.
3. Stir in flour until smooth and gradually add in milk. Cook over direct heat, stirring constantly until sauce boils and thickens. This sauce is good as an accompaniment for fish, eggs, meat loaves, or croquettes.

« RED CHERRY TOPPING »

1 ¼ cups dehydrated sour pie cherries
2 cups water
¾ cup sugar

2 tablespoons cornstarch
½ teaspoon almond extract

1. Soak cherries in water until reconstituted, then cook over medium heat until tender. Drain and chill, reserving syrup for use later.
2. Mix together sugar, cornstarch, and reserved cooled syrup. Cook over medium heat, stirring often until thick and clear.
3. Add in almond extract and cherries, stirring thoroughly. Serve hot or cold over Cottage Pudding Batter (pg. 88), pour into baked pie shell or pie tarts, or pour over white cake and serve with whipped cream.

« STEWED SOUR RED CHERRY PANCAKE OR PUDDING SAUCE »

Yield: 5–6 servings

2 ½ cups dehydrated sour pie cherries
2 ½ cups water
1 cup sugar
dash of salt

1 ½ teaspoons cornstarch
2 tablespoons butter
1–2 drops almond extract

1. Soak cherries in water until reconstituted, then simmer until tender. Add sugar and salt. Cook 10 minutes longer, stirring occasionally. Cool.
2. Blend 2 tablespoons juice from stewed cherries smoothly with cornstarch. Stir into cherries and cook with constant stirring until sauce is thickened and clear.
3. Remove from heat; stir in butter and almond extract. Serve warm as sauce or as a simple dessert.

Stewed sour red cherries make a delicious topping for pancakes.

« PLUM SAUCE »

2 cups dehydrated plums
2 cups plus 3 tablespoons (cold) water
2 tablespoons cornstarch

¼ teaspoon salt
1⁄16 teaspoon allspice
2 tablespoons lemon juice

1. Soak plums in 2 cups of water until reconstituted. Drain off liquid; there should be approximately 1 ½ cups. If not, add water to make 1 ½ cups. Heat juice to boiling with 1 small piece of stick cinnamon. Cut plums into bite-sized pieces.
2. Mix together cornstarch, salt, and 3 tablespoons of cold water. Add to boiling juice. Stir constantly until mixture boils again and is thickened.
3. Add in allspice, lemon juice, and plums. Simmer slowly 10 minutes. Serve hot over ham loaf or loaf slices.

« TOMATO SAUCE »

Yield: 2–2 ¼ cups

3 ½ cups dehydrated tomatoes
½ cup dehydrated onions
¼ cup dehydrated carrots
¼ cup dehydrated green peppers
6 cups water
3 tablespoons vegetable oil

1 small clove garlic
1 medium bay leaf
½ cup dehydrated celery leaves
½ teaspoon salt
pepper to taste
1 teaspoon sugar

1. Soak tomatoes in 4 cups of water until reconstituted. Soak onions in 1 cup of water until reconstituted. Soak carrots in ½ cup water until reconstituted. Soak green peppers in ½ cup water until reconstituted. Drain vegetables, reserving liquid from reconstituted tomatoes.
2. Heat the vegetable oil, then add in garlic, drained onion, green peppers, and carrots in saucepan. Sauté until onion turns a golden color, stirring constantly, then add in tomatoes and reserved liquid. Cover and cook slowly with occasional stirring until sauce thickens, about 40–45 minutes.
3. Add in sugar, salt, and pepper to taste. Simmer 5 more minutes, then rub mixture through fine sieve. Excellent on spaghetti, ravioli, or omelet.

Tomato sauce has a variety of uses: try putting it on fish, beans, or eggs.

« TOMATO PASTE »

1. Use firm, ripe red tomatoes. Wash thoroughly and crush. Place in a vessel and cook over medium heat until peelings begin to loosen. When peels have loosened, force tomatoes through a sieve. Let stand for 15–20 minutes, then pour off free surface moisture (use it in soups, etc.).
2. Cook remaining pulp and liquid over medium heat until it is as concentrated as heavy cream, stirring frequently to prevent sticking and scorching. Pour into shallow pan and place pans in dryer. Dry until paste leaves edges of pan and begins to curl; be sure center of paste is dry.
3. Roll paste as a jelly roll. Cut into lengths to fit airtight, moisture tight container.

« SEASONED TOMATO PASTE »

4 quarts ripe tomatoes
2 tablespoons minced basil leaves
2 teaspoons salt
½ cup chopped celery
½ cup chopped carrots

⅓ cup onion slices
½ teaspoon ground cinnamon
½ teaspoon pepper
½ teaspoon ground cloves

1. Combine all ingredients in a preserving kettle. Simmer until ingredients are soft. Strain through a sieve. Cook puree until very thick.
2. Spread in shallow pans. Dehydrate until no evidence of moisture remains. Pack carefully in airtight, moisture tight containers.

« WHITE SAUCE »

Yield: about 1 cup

Thin	Medium	Thick
1 tablespoon butter	2 tablespoons butter	3 or 4 tablespoons butter
1 tablespoon flour	2 tablespoons flour	3 or 4 tablespoons flour
½ teaspoon salt	½ teaspoon salt	½ teaspoon salt
1 cup milk	1 cup milk	1 cup milk

1. Melt butter in saucepan, add flour and salt, then blend mixture until smooth. Stir in cold milk gradually and cook over direct heat, stirring constantly until sauce boils and becomes thick and smooth. If stirring is done carefully, there will be no lumping, but white sauce that has lumped may often be smoothed by beating with a rotary beater.
2. If it is necessary to keep white sauce warm more than a few minutes before using, place over boiling water and keep it covered, stirring occasionally.

CHAPTER XXI
« FRUIT-FLAVORED MILKSHAKE RECIPES »

« BANANA SHAKE »

Yield: 1–2 servings

½ cup dehydrated bananas
½ cup water
1 cup milk
⅓ cup orange juice

1 teaspoon sugar
1 large scoop ice cream
dash of salt

1. Soak bananas in water until reconstituted.
2. Pour milk into shaker or mixing bowl and add drained mashed reconstituted bananas, orange juice, sugar, ice cream, and salt. Shake or beat well. Serve at once.

Yield: 1 serving

⅓ cup dehydrated peaches	dash of salt
⅓ cup water	2–3 drops almond extract
⅓ cup milk	1 large scoop vanilla ice cream

1. Soak peaches in water until reconstituted, then mash thoroughly.
2. Put mashed peaches and water into shaker or mixing bowl, and add milk, salt, almond extract, and ice cream. Shake or beat well. Serve at once.

Yield: 2 servings

½ cup dehydrated prunes	dash of salt
½ cup water	1 teaspoon lemon juice
⅓ cup orange juice	1 tablespoon sugar
1 cup milk	1 large scoop vanilla ice cream

1. Soak prunes in water until reconstituted, then put prunes and water in blender and make a puree.
2. Pour puree into shaker or mixing bowl and add in the orange juice, milk, salt, lemon juice, sugar, and ice cream. Shake or beat well. Serve at once.

CHAPTER XXII
« Soup Recipes »

« CREAM OF CARROT SOUP »

Yield: 5 servings

2 cups dehydrated carrots
4 ¼ cups water
1 teaspoon dehydrated onion
2 tablespoons butter

5 tablespoons flour
1 ⅔ cups evaporated milk
1 teaspoon salt

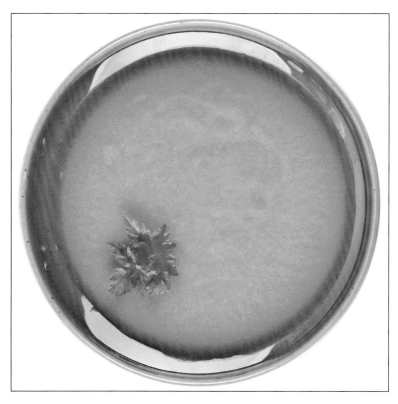

Cream of carrot soup.

1. Soak carrots in 4 cups of water until reconstituted. Cook over medium heat until carrots are tender, approximately 35 minutes. Drain off liquid (reserve this liquid) and put cooked drained carrots through a sieve, ricer, or food mill.
2. Soak onions in ¼ cup of water until reconstituted, then drain off water.
3. Melt butter in saucepan and add in onions. Cook until soft, then blend in flour.
4. Measure liquid drained off carrots; there should be at least 1 ¼ cups; if less, add additional fresh water; if more, discard the additional. Add the evaporated milk and cook over direct heat, stirring constantly until mixture boils and thickens.
5. Add in the carrots and salt. Reheat soup and serve piping hot with crisp crackers or croutons.

« CREAM OF CELERY SOUP »

Yield: 5 servings

2 tablespoons dehydrated onions
1 cup dehydrated celery
1 cup water
½ teaspoon plus 1 ¼ teaspoons salt

¼ cup butter or margarine
¼ cup flour
1 quart milk

1. Soak onions and celery in water until reconstituted, then cook over medium heat until tender. Add ½ teaspoon salt and stir.
2. Melt butter or margarine in saucepan, then blend in flour and gradually add in milk. Cook with constant stirring until sauce boils and thickens.
3. Add 1 ¼ teaspoons salt to cooked vegetables and their liquid and reheat to boiling. Garnish with chopped parsley. A chopped or diced hard-boiled egg is also an attractive and nutritious garnish.

« CREAM OF ONION SOUP »

Yield: 5 servings

¾ cup dehydrated onions
3 cups water
2 slices bacon
2 tablespoons flour

1 ⅔ cups evaporated milk
1 teaspoon salt or to taste
pepper to taste

1. Soak onions in 1 cup water until reconstituted; drain, reserving liquid for later.
2. Chop bacon into fine pieces, place in soup kettle, and fry until just done. Add drained onions and flour and stir until flour is blended with drippings.

3. Gradually add in reserved liquid plus two cups of water and stir thoroughly until mixture is smooth. Cover and simmer until onion is tender, about 15 minutes. Add evaporated milk, salt, and pepper.

4. Reheat, uncovered, to boiling. Place a slice of toast in the bottom of each soup bowl and pour hot soup over it and serve immediately.

« CREAM OF PEA SOUP »

Yield: 5 servings

1 ¼ cups dehydrated peas
½ teaspoon dehydrated onions
2 cups water
1 ½ teaspoons sugar

1 teaspoon salt
White Sauce
10–15 croutons

1. Soak peas and onions in water until reconstituted. Drain liquid, measure, and add cold water to make 2 cups liquid. Place liquid and peas in a saucepan. Place over heat and cook until peas are tender. Add sugar and salt and simmer for 5 more minutes.

2. When hot, rub through a food mill or sieve. There should be 2 ½ cups puree and liquid. Combine with hot White Sauce (pg. 132), reheat, and serve hot. Float 2 or 3 croutons on each portion just before serving.

« CREAM OF POTATO SOUP »

Yield: 5 servings

2 cups diced dehydrated potatoes
¼ cup dehydrated onions
¼ cup dehydrated celery
¼ cup dehydrated green pepper
1 small whole red pepper pod
4–5 cups water

1 tablespoon butter
1 cup evaporated milk
salt to taste
pepper to taste
1 teaspoon dried parsley

1. Put vegetables and water in a large pan, bring to a boil, and simmer until tender. When vegetables are tender, mash potatoes somewhat with potato masher.

2. Add in butter, milk, salt, pepper, and parsley. When mixed thoroughly and heated throughout, take out the whole red pepper pod and serve hot.

« CREAM OF SPINACH SOUP »

Yield: 5 servings

2 ½ cups dehydrated spinach or Swiss
    chard
2 tablespoons dehydrated onions
4 cups water
1 ½ teaspoons flour

3 cups chicken broth or 3 bouillon cubes
    dissolved in 3 cups hot water
½ cup fresh spinach, finely chopped
1 cup cream

1. Soak spinach or Swiss chard and onions in water until reconstituted. When reconstituted, drain; reserve liquid.
2. Blend flour and 3 tablespoons of the reserved liquid into a paste. Add in chicken broth or bouillons cubes and 3 cups of reserved water. Cook over direct heat, stirring constantly until mixture boils.
3. Add spinach and cream. Reheat to scalding and serve piping hot with croutons or crisp crackers.

« CREAM OF TOMATO SOUP »

Yield: 5 servings

3 cups dehydrated tomatoes
1 tablespoon dehydrated parsley
1 tablespoon dehydrated onions
3 cups water
6 whole cloves

½ bay leaf
¾ teaspoon whole black peppers
2 teaspoons sugar
¾ teaspoons salt

1. Soak tomatoes, parsley, and onions in water until reconstituted. Transfer vegetables and liquid to a saucepan and add cloves, bay leaf, pepper, sugar, and salt. Heat to boiling, then reduce heat and simmer for five minutes.
2. Rub mixture through a food mill or sieve. Have White Sauce (pg. 132) thoroughly heated in another pan. When ready to serve, combine by stirring the hot tomato puree slowly into the hot white sauce. Serve immediately.

« CREAM OF VEGETABLE SOUP »

Yield: 5 servings

½ cup dehydrated potatoes
2 tablespoons dehydrated onions
¼ cup dehydrated carrots
⅛ cup dehydrated celery leaves
2 cups water

3 tablespoons butter, margarine, or
  bacon fat
2 tablespoons flour
1 quart milk

1. Soak potatoes, onions, carrots, and celery leaves in water until reconstituted. When they are reconstituted to their normal size, drain, reserving liquid, and chop or dice vegetables fine.
2. Melt butter, margarine, or bacon fat in pan, then add in 1 cup of reserved liquid. Cover and simmer for 10 minutes, stirring occasionally.
3. Blend together flour and milk. Heat to boiling, stirring constantly. Add to vegetables. Add seasonings and serve at once.

« DILL-GREEN BEAN SOUP »

¼ cup dehydrated onions
1 cup dehydrated green beans
½ cup dehydrated potatoes
4 ¼ cups water
1–2 tablespoons dill weed or seed,
  crushed

1 clove of garlic (optional)
2–3 tablespoons flour
salt to taste
pepper to taste

1. Soak onions in ¼ cup water for 5–10 minutes, then sauté onion with dill weed or dill seed. Add in flour and cook until golden brown.
2. Add 4 cups of water, green beans, and potatoes and simmer 1 ½ hours or until beans are tender. Add salt and pepper and serve hot.

« CABBAGE-RICE SOUP »

Yield: 4 servings

2 tablespoons dehydrated onion
1 ½ cups dehydrated cabbage
1 ¾ cups water
2 tablespoons butter or margarine
¼ cup raw rice

4 chicken bouillon cubes
½ teaspoon salt
1 tablespoon of grated cheese
dash of paprika

1. Soak onions in ¼ cup water until reconstituted; drain, and reserve liquid. Soak cabbage in 1 ½ cups water until reconstituted; drain, and reserve liquid. Pour reserved liquid into a measuring cup and add in water until you have 1 quart.
2. Melt butter or margarine in saucepan and add drained onions. Sauté for 5 minutes, then add in rice, 1 quart water, and bouillon cubes. Simmer 15 minutes.
3. Add in drained cabbage and cook uncovered another 5 minutes. Add salt and cook another 5 minutes. Sprinkle grated cheese on top of each serving, then add the paprika. Serve immediately.

« HAMBURGER SOUP »

Yield: 4 servings

1 pound hamburger	⅓ cup dehydrated green beans (optional)
3 beef bouillon cubes	⅓ cup dehydrated corn (optional)
5 cups hot water	½ teaspoon thyme
½ cup dehydrated onions	10 peppercorns
1 cup dehydrated carrots	1 bay leaf
½ cup dehydrated celery tops	2 tablespoons dehydrated parsley
2 cups dehydrated tomatoes and 1 cup of water or 1 quart fresh tomatoes	1 ½ cups cooked heavy crinkle noodles or 1 ½ cups cooked elbow macaroni

1. Brown hamburger and drain when done. Put cooked hamburger in large kettle and add everything but the noodles.
2. Cook about 45 minutes or until tender. Add in noodles and stir, then serve hot.

Note: This is a thick soup; more water may be added if necessary.

« PEA AND RICE SOUP »

Yield: 4 servings

½ cup dehydrated peas	2 ½ cups milk
½ tablespoon dehydrated onions	1 teaspoon salt
1 cup water	1 tablespoon dehydrated parsley
¼ cup converted or enriched rice	½ teaspoon dehydrated celery leaves
2 chicken bouillon cubes	1 tablespoon butter

1. Soak peas and onions in water until reconstituted. Cook until tender; then drain and reserve liquid. Add enough water to reserved liquid to equal 3 cups and boil.

2. Put rice and reserved, boiling water in double boiler. Cook rice according to directions on box until tender.
3. Add in reconstituted and cooked peas and onions, boullion cubes, milk, salt, parsley, celery leaves, and butter. Stir thoroughly and place over boiling water to reheat thoroughly.

« SPLIT PEA SOUP »

Yield: 12 servings

1 pound green split peas
3 quarts fresh water
1 pound pure pork sausage
½ cup dehydrated diced celery

½ cup dehydrated diced onions
½ cup dehydrated diced potatoes
flour

1. Soak peas for 15 minutes, then drain. Cook peas in 3 quarts of water.
2. Roll sausage into 1-inch balls and roll them in flour, then add them to the peas. Cook soup until sausage is done.
3. Add celery, onions, and potatoes and cook slowly for several hours. Serve when vegetables have reconstituted.

« POTATO-CARROT SOUP »

Yield: 5 servings

2 cups dehydrated potatoes
1 cup dehydrated carrots
½ cup dehydrated onions
4 cups water
2 teaspoons salt

1 ⅔ cups cream or evaporated milk
dash cayenne
dash celery salt
dash paprika

1. Soak potatoes, carrots, and onions in water until reconstituted. After reconstitution, cook until tender, about 30 minutes. Drain and measure liquid. There should be 1 ¾ cups liquid left.
2. Put reserved liquid and reconstituted vegetables into a saucepan and add in salt and cream or evaporated milk.
3. Heat just to scalding, then add in cayenne and celery salt.
4. Reheat and serve at once, adding a dash of paprika on top of each serving.

« RICE AND SPINACH SOUP »

Yield: 4 servings

4 cups dehydrated spinach or Swiss chard	1 quart boiling water
1 tablespoon dehydrated onions	2 teaspoons salt
4 cups plus 1 quart water	2 cups milk
⅓ cup brown rice	2 tablespoons margarine

1. Soak spinach or Swiss chard and onions in water until reconstituted, then simmer until tender.
2. Put 1 quart of water in a pot and boil. When boiling, add in rice and salt. Cook uncovered until rice is thoroughly tender, about 40–45 minutes.
3. Add in milk, drained vegetables, and margarine. Simmer for 10 minutes. Serve at once with a sprinkling of paprika on each bowl for garnish.

« VEGETABLE SOUPS »

Any combination of vegetables is delicious in making hearty soups. Here is one example.
Yield: approximately 4 cups

¼ cup dehydrated cabbage	½ cup dehydrated potatoes
¼ cup dehydrated onions	5 cups of water
¼ cup dehydrated celery	2 bouillon cubes
¼ cup dehydrated carrots	½ teaspoon salt or to taste

1. Put water and vegetables in pan and soak until vegetables are reconstituted, then simmer until vegetables are tender, approximately 1 ½ hours.
2. Add in bouillon cubes and salt, then simmer 10 minutes more.

Note: Cooked dehydrated beef or chicken chunks may be added to the vegetables as they are reconstituting.
Note: Use either chicken or beef bouillon cubes.

Use any combination of vegetables you like to make a hearty, tasty soup.

CHAPTER XXIII

« VEGETABLE RECIPES »

« BUTTERED OR CREAMED GREEN BEANS »

Yield: 4–5 servings

2 cups dehydrated green beans
2 cups water
½ teaspoon salt

1 teaspoon sugar
Melted butter or Medium White Sauce
  (pg. 132)

1. Soak green beans in water until reconstituted, then cook over medium heat until tender.
2. Add salt, cook 5 minutes more, then drain off liquid. Add in sugar and either butter or Medium White Sauce and serve immediately.

Buttered green beans make an excellent side dish.

« GREEN BEANS AU GRATIN »

Yield: 5 servings

1 cup dehydrated green beans
1 cup water
5 slices bacon
2 tablespoons flour

½ cup milk
¾ cup grated sharp cheese
½ cup rolled cornflakes or bread crumbs
2 tablespoons butter, melted

1. Soak green beans in water until reconstituted, then cook over medium heat until almost tender. Drain, reserving liquid.
2. Pan-broil the bacon and drain off fat, then place bacon on paper towels to catch remaining fat.
3. Measure 3 tablespoons of the drippings and return to skillet. Add in flour and stir until blended, then add in reserved liquid. Stir constantly over direct heat until sauce boils and thickens.
4. When sauce has thickened, add beans and grated cheese, then pour into a buttered 6-cup casserole dish.
5. Mix together cornflakes or bread crumbs with melted butter, then sprinkle over beans and cheese.
6. Bake at 325°F for about 20 minutes or until browned and thoroughly heated through. Two minutes before removing from oven, sprinkle with the chopped crisp bacon.

« GREEN BEANS IN EGG SAUCE »

Yield: 4 servings

1 ½ cups dehydrated green beans
3 cups water
2 tablespoons margarine
2 tablespoons flour
½ cup milk

⅛ teaspoon celery seed
¼ teaspoon salt
dash pepper
3 hard-boiled sliced eggs

1. Soak green beans in water until reconstituted, then cook over medium heat until tender. Drain, reserving ½ cup liquid.
2. Melt margarine in saucepan and add in flour. Stir together, then slowly add in milk and reserved liquid.
3. Stir constantly; cook until mixture bubbles and becomes thickened, then add in celery salt, salt, and pepper. Stir well. Fold eggs in gently.
4. Reheat sauce and pour over hot beans placed in a pre-warmed serving dish. Serve immediately.

« GREEN BEANS BAKED LUCETTE »

Yield: 6 servings

2 cups dehydrated cut green beans
½ cup dehydrated onions
4 cups water

½ teaspoon salt
1 can cream of mushroom soup
½ cup grated cheese

1. Soak green beans and onions in water until reconstituted, then simmer until green beans are tender. Add in salt, then simmer 5 minutes more. Drain, reserving ¼ cup liquid.
2. Mix cream of mushroom soup with reserved liquid.
3. Alternate layers of drained beans and onions and soup mixture in baking dish.
4. Sprinkle with cheese and bake at 350°F for 30 minutes.

« GREEN BEANS AND SAUCE »

Yield: 6 servings

2 cups cut green beans
4 cups water
½ teaspoon salt

1 can cream of mushroom soup
½ cup grated cheese

1. Simmer green beans in water until tender, then add in salt and simmer 5 minutes more. Drain, reserving ¼ cup liquid.
2. Mix cream of mushroom soup with reserved liquid.
3. Alternate layers of drained and soup mixture in baking dish.
4. Sprinkle with cheese and bake at 350°F for 30 minutes.

« BEETS DE LUXE »

Yield: 4 servings

1 cup dehydrated red beets
1 cup water plus 2 tablespoons cold water
1 teaspoon grated onion
¼ teaspoon salt

2 teaspoons cornstarch
¼ cup bread crumbs
1 tablespoon melted butter
1 ½ ounces grated Parmesan cheese
¼ cup chopped parsley

1. Soak beets in water until reconstituted, then cover and cook over medium heat until tender. Add onion and salt.

2. Blend together cornstarch and cold water until paste forms, then add to beets, stirring well. Cook until mixture boils and thickens. Pour beets into a serving dish.
3. Mix bread crumbs in melted butter and toast, then sprinkle over beets. Spread cheese and parsley over top and serve at once.

« BEETS IN ORANGE SAUCE »

Yield: 4 servings

1 ½ cups dehydrated, shredded red beets
1 ½ cups water
3 tablespoons sugar
2 tablespoons cornstarch
¼ teaspoon salt

½ cup orange juice
¼ cup lemon juice
⅛ teaspoon orange rind
⅛ teaspoon lemon rind

1. Soak beets in water until reconstituted, then cover and cook over medium heat until tender. Drain.
2. Blend the sugar, cornstarch, salt, lemon juice, and orange juice together in top of a double boiler. Cook over boiling water until thick and transparent, stirring constantly.
3. When thickened, add in the lemon rind, orange rind, and cooked, drained beets. Mix lightly. Cook over boiling water until thoroughly heated. Serve at once.

« SLICED BEETS WITH LEMON JUICE »

Yield: 10–12 servings

3 cups sliced dehydrated beets
6 cups plus 4 tablespoons water
dash of nutmeg
1 cup sugar
2 tablespoons butter

2 tablespoons whole cloves
4 sticks cinnamon
2–3 lemons, juiced
2 tablespoons cornstarch

1. Simmer beets in 6 cups of water until tender. Drain, reserving 2 cups of liquid.
2. Put cloves, cinnamon, and nutmeg in a cheesecloth bag and tie closed. Place bag in reserved liquid. Cook 2–3 minutes. Add in sugar, butter, lemon juice, and drained beets. Cook 2 minutes.
3. Take out spice bag and pour off juice into another pan.
4. Add cornstarch and 4 tablespoons of water to juice. Mix together well and cook for 2 minutes before pouring over beets. Heat and serve.

Note: Color the mixture if needed. Seasonings must be to taste. The sauce tastes better if allowed to stand a day or so.

« BEETS WITH SOUR SAUCE »

Yield: 4 servings

1 ½ cups dehydrated red beets
1 ½ cups water
2 tablespoons butter or margarine
2 tablespoons flour
¾ cup milk

2 tablespoons vinegar
½ teaspoon sugar
¼ teaspoon salt
dash of pepper

1. Soak beets in water until reconstituted, then cover and cook over medium heat until tender; drain.
2. Melt butter or margarine in saucepan and blend in flour. When mixed, gradually add in milk. Stir until mixture is smooth and thickened, then add in vinegar, sugar, salt, and pepper.
3. Serve over the hot drained beets.

« RUBY RED BEETS »

Yield: 4 servings

1 ½ cups dehydrated red beets
1 ½ cups water
½ teaspoon onion juice
2 tablespoons lemon juice

⅜ teaspoon salt
2 teaspoons sugar
½ cup sour cream

1. Soak beets in water until reconstituted, then cover and cook over medium heat until tender; drain. Cool beets and slice into slivers.
2. Mix together onion juice, lemon juice, salt, sugar, and sour cream, then add in slivered beets. Toss lightly to blend seasonings. Serve warm or chilled.

« CABBAGE AU GRATIN »

Yield: 5 servings

5 cups dehydrated cabbage
5 cups water
1 teaspoon salt
3 tablespoons butter
3 tablespoons flour

¼ cup evaporated milk
1 ½ cups grated cheese
½ cup fine dry bread crumbs
2 tablespoons butter, melted

1. Soak cabbage in water until reconstituted, then cover and cook over medium heat until just tender, about 7 minutes. Add salt, cook 1 minute longer, then drain, reserving ¾ cup water.
2. Melt butter in saucepan, then add in flour. When mixed, gradually add in evaporated milk and reserved liquid. Stir constantly until sauce boils and thickens; add salt to taste.
3. Place a layer of cooked cabbage in bottom of a buttered casserole dish, pour part of the sauce over it, then sprinkle with some cheese. Repeat until all ingredients are used, ending with cheese on top.
4. Mix bread crumbs in melted butter and sprinkle on top of casserole. Bake at 350°F for 20 minutes or until nicely browned.

« ROTKOHL-RED CABBAGE »

Yield: 4 servings

2 cups dried cabbage
2 cups water
1 tablespoon oil
⅓ cup vinegar

3 tablespoons sugar or brown sugar
pinch allspice
salt to taste
2 tablespoons cornstarch

1. Mix together the cabbage and water, and let stand for 30 minutes. Add in oil, vinegar, sugar, allspice, and salt to taste.
2. Cook until tender, thickening with cornstarch.

« KRAUT FLECKLA »

1 cup dehydrated cabbage	wide noodles
2 cups water	1–2 tablespoons butter

1. Soak cabbage in water for 20 minutes, then drain.
2. Cook homemade wide noodles or commercially-made heavy wide noodles. Drain well.
3. Sauté cabbage in butter until light brown—just a very few minutes. Add noodles and salt lightly to taste.
4. Serve with jam, elderberry syrup, or sugar. Simple but delicious.

« BUTTERED CARROTS »

Yield: approximately 5 servings

1 cup dehydrated carrots	2 tablespoons butter
2 cups water	chopped dehydrated parsley
½ teaspoon salt	

Buttered carrots are a tasty addition to any meal.

1. Soak carrots in water until reconstituted, then cook over moderate heat until tender, approximately 30 minutes. Add salt and simmer 5 minutes more.
2. Remove cover to evaporate remaining liquid, watching carefully to avoid scorching. Add butter and sprinkle on parsley.

« CREAMED CARROTS »

Add 2 cups Medium White Sauce (pg. 132) to above Buttered Carrots.

« CARROTS »

Soak dehydrated carrots in cold water until crisp. Carrots can now be used in salads.

« SEASONED CARROTS »

2 cups dehydrated carrots
1 tablespoon dehydrated onions
4 cups water

2 tablespoons butter
1 ¾ teaspoons seasoned salt

1. Simmer the carrots and onions together until tender.
2. Add butter and seasoned salt, and simmer until ingredients are well blended.

« CANDIED CARROTS »

Yield: 14–16 servings

4 cups dehydrated carrots
8 cups water
3 tablespoons butter

4 tablespoons brown sugar
¼ teaspoon salt

1. Mix carrots and water and simmer until carrots are done. Drain off water, reserving 4 tablespoons.
2. Put reserved liquid in another saucepan and add butter, brown sugar, and salt. Cook for 2 minutes.
3. Pour cooked carrots into the saucepan and then carefully back, repeating until they are well coated.

« CREAMED CARROTS AND CELERY »

Yield: 5 servings

1 cup dehydrated carrots	2 tablespoons butter or margarine
½ cup dehydrated celery	3 tablespoons flour
2 cups water	1 cup thin cream or evaporated milk

1. Soak carrots and celery in water until reconstituted, then cover and cook until tender; drain, saving water. Measure water and, if necessary, boil rapidly to concentrate to 1 cup.
2. Melt butter or margarine in saucepan and blend in flour. Mix well, then add in cream or evaporated milk and reserved liquid.
3. Reheat thoroughly. Serve the creamed vegetables poured over toast.

« CARROT SOUFFLÉ »

Yield: 5 servings

1 cup dehydrated carrots	1 cup milk
2 cups water	1 teaspoon salt
1 tablespoon butter or margarine plus	dash of pepper
2 tablespoons melted butter	3 egg yolks, beaten
4 tablespoons flour	3 egg whites, stiffly beaten

1. Soak carrots in water until reconstituted. Drain off water, reserving ¼ cup liquid. Shred carrots.
2. Put shredded carrots, reserved liquid, and 1 tablespoon of butter or margarine in saucepan. Cover and cook slowly 10 minutes. Cool.
3. In second saucepan, mix 2 tablespoons of butter with flour. Blend well and add in milk, salt, and pepper. When mixed, stir in egg yolks and carrot mixture, then fold in egg whites.
4. Place carefully into casserole. Bake about 40 minutes at 375°F. Serve at once.

« CARROTS IN ORANGE SAUCE »

Yield: 4 servings

½ cup dehydrated carrots	1 ½ tablespoons sugar
1 cup water	½ cup orange juice
⅓ teaspoon salt	1 tablespoon or more coconut milk
2 teaspoons cornstarch	1 tablespoon butter

1. Soak carrots in water until reconstituted, then cook over moderate heat until tender.
2. Mix salt, cornstarch, sugar, and orange juice until smooth and add to carrots. Cook and stir until thickened and clear.
3. When thick, add in coconut milk and butter. Reheat to boiling. Serve hot.

« BUTTERED CELERY »

Yield: approximately 5 servings

1 ½ cups dehydrated celery   ¼ teaspoon salt
3 cups water   2–3 tablespoons butter, melted

1. Soak celery in water until reconstituted, then cook at moderate heat until tender, about 15–20 minutes.
2. Add salt and simmer 5 more minutes.
3. Drain celery and add melted butter.

« CREAMED CELERY »

Prepare celery as directed above for Buttered Celery, but substitute 2 cups Thin or Medium White Sauce (pg. 132) in place of the butter.

« BUTTERED CORN »

Yield: approximately 5 servings

2 cups dehydrated corn   2–3 tablespoons butter
4 cups water   salt to taste

1. Soak corn in water until reconstituted, then cook over medium heat until completely tender.
2. Add salt and butter. Heat until butter is melted and most of water has evaporated.

« CORN CHOWDER »

Yield: 8 cups

Use dehydrated vegetables and follow directions for reconstituting as found on pg. 53–55.

1 ½ cups dehydrated potatoes, reconstituted
2 tablespoons dehydrated onions, reconstituted
½ cup dehydrated celery, reconstituted
2 cups boiling water
¼ pound bacon

⅓ pound mushrooms, sliced
2 tablespoons dehydrated peppers, reconstituted
1 can cream style yellow corn
3 cups milk
2 ½ teaspoons salt
dash of pepper

1. Put the potatoes, onions, celery, and water in top of 2 ½-quart double boiler. Heat to boiling over direct heat, cover, reduce heat and simmer for 10 minutes.
2. Meanwhile, pan-fry bacon and drain on paper towels. Sauté the mushrooms and the peppers in bacon drippings for 5 minutes. And in creamed corn, milk, salt, and pepper.
3. Add cooked vegetables and thin liquid. Reheat over boiling water. Stir gently to mix well. Serve piping hot and garnish with the bacon bits.

« CREAMED CORN WITH GREEN PEPPER »

Yield: 4 servings

1 ½ cups dehydrated corn
2 tablespoons dehydrated green pepper
2 tablespoons dehydrated onions

3 ½ cups water
2 tablespoons butter
½ cup milk

1. Soak corn in 3 cups of water until reconstituted. Soak peppers in ¼ cup water until reconstituted. Soak onions in ¼ cup water until reconstituted. When above vegetables are reconstituted, drain, reserving ¾ cup liquid.
2. Melt butter in saucepan and add in drained corn, drained onion, and reserved liquid. Cover and simmer until water is almost evaporated and the kernels are tender.
3. When the water has almost evaporated, add in drained peppers and milk. Cook 5 minutes more; serve at once.

« FRESH CORN RABBIT »

Yield: 4 servings

¾ cups dehydrated corn	1 teaspoon salt
2 cups dehydrated tomatoes	⅛ teaspoon pepper
2 ¼ cups water	1 teaspoon sugar
1 tablespoon chopped onions	½ teaspoon Worcestershire sauce
2 tablespoons chopped green pepper	½ pound American cheese cut in ¼-inch
3 tablespoons butter or margarine	cubes
1 tablespoon flour	2 eggs, beaten

1. Soak corn and tomatoes in 2 cups of water until reconstituted. Soak onions and peppers in ¼ cup water until reconstituted. Drain water from reconstituted corn and tomatoes, reserving ¼ cup liquid. Put corn, tomatoes, and ¼ cup reserved liquid in top of double boiler.
2. Melt butter or margarine in saucepan and add in drained onions and peppers. Sauté until onions are slightly transparent.
3. Add and blend in the flour, then combine it with tomato mixture and heat just to boiling. Place over boiling water.
4. Add in salt, pepper, sugar, Worcestershire sauce, and cheese. Stir until cheese melts.
5. Pour a small amount of hot mixture into beaten eggs. Beat, return to double boiler, and stir for 2 minutes. Serve piping hot on slices of lightly buttered toast.

« ONIONS »

Use ¼ the amount of dried onions as is called for in any recipe. They can be put into soups and will reconstitute completely. They must have liquid of some type simmered with them to make sure they reconstitute. Powder them in a blender and use the onion powder to sprinkle over hamburgers, etc., as they are cooking. Use only a small amount since onion powder is very concentrated. Onion powder can also be sprinkled over salads. Onions can be and are used in many of the recipes in this book.

Dried onions can be used in a variety of recipes.

« BUTTERED OR CREAMED PEAS »

Yield: 5 servings

2 cups dehydrated peas	½ teaspoon salt
4 cups water	2–3 tablespoons butter

1. Soak peas in water until reconstituted, then cook over medium heat until tender. Add salt and cook 5 minutes longer.
2. Drain liquid off if necessary; pour melted butter or a Thin White Sauce (pg. 132) over them and serve immediately.

Note: Equal quantities of reconstituted, drained, and cooked peas, cauliflower, or celery may be combined and buttered.

« CREAMED PEAS AND NEW POTATOES »

Yield: 4 servings

2 cups dehydrated potatoes	2 tablespoons dehydrated radishes
¾ cup dehydrated peas	1 ¼ teaspoons salt
1 teaspoon dehydrated onions	½ cup evaporated milk
4 ¼ cups water	2 tablespoons butter

1. Soak potatoes, peas, and onions in 4 cups of water until reconstituted.
2. Cook the reconstituted potatoes, peas, and onions until tender, approximately 30 minutes. Drain off liquid, reserving ½ cup.
3. Soak radishes in ¼ cup water until reconstituted. Drain.

4. Add the salt, evaporated milk, butter, and reserved liquid to cooked vegetables. Simmer very slowly until liquid is somewhat thickened. Add the drained radishes just before serving.

« POTATOES AU GRATIN »

Yield: 5 servings

5 ½ cups dehydrated potatoes   2 cups Thin White Sauce
6 cups water   2 cups grated cheese

1. Soak potatoes in water until reconstituted, then drain. Combine drained reconstituted potatoes and 2 cups Thin White Sauce (pg. 132) in saucepan and heat gently until sauce bubbles.
2. Arrange layers of the creamed potatoes in a buttered casserole with grated cheese between layers and on top.
3. Cover casserole, and bake at 375°F until potatoes are tender, about 30 minutes. Then remove cover and brown the surface, either in oven with temperature increased to 475°F or under broiler.

Note: For variation in color and flavor, add reconstituted drained green pepper or pimento, or both, to the creamed potatoes just before placing into the casserole.

« POTATOES IN CARAWAY SAUCE »

Yield: 4 servings

4 cups dehydrated potatoes
4 cups water
1 cup sour cream

1 ¼ teaspoons salt
½ teaspoon caraway seeds
parsley

1. Soak potatoes in water until reconstituted. After reconstitution, cook over medium heat until tender. Drain off any remaining water.
2. Combine sour cream, salt, and caraway seeds. Pour this mixture over the drained potatoes and heat for 2 minutes, turning the potatoes in the sauce as it heats.
3. Transfer to a hot serving dish and garnish with parsley.

« POTATO CHEESE PUFFS »

Yield: 4 servings

2 cups dehydrated potatoes
4 cups water
¼ cup milk
2 eggs, yolks and whites separated
¾ cup grated cheese

1 ½ teaspoons salt
1 ½ teaspoons fresh onion juice (or onion powder)
1 tablespoon dehydrated parsley

1. Soak potatoes in water until reconstituted. After reconstituting, cook over medium heat until potatoes are tender, then drain off remaining liquid. Using a ricer, rice potatoes while hot into a bowl.
2. Add in milk, egg yolks, grated cheese, salt, onion juice, and parsley. Whip until fluffy.
3. Beat egg whites until stiff, then fold into the potato mixture. Pile lightly into 8 mounds on a greased cookie sheet or shallow pan. Bake 15–20 minutes at 375°F. Serve immediately while still puffy.

« POTATO CROQUETTES »

Yield: 9 croquettes

A plate full of freshly baked potato croquettes.

5 cups dehydrated potatoes	dash of pepper
6 cups plus 1 tablespoon water	1 ¼ teaspoons onion powder or grated
⅓ cup butter or margarine	onion
1 teaspoon salt	1 egg, beaten
⅓ cup milk	2 cups bread crumbs

1. Soak potatoes in 6 cups water until reconstituted. After reconstitution, cook until tender. If water has not completely evaporated, drain off excess. Put potatoes through food mill or ricer.
2. Return potatoes to pan and add butter or margarine, salt, and milk. Beat until light and fluffy. Potatoes for croquettes should be quite stiff and hold together well. Stir in pepper and onion powder.
3. Cool to room temperature. Measure ⅓ cup portions onto waxed paper spread with buttered bread crumbs. Shape croquettes into cones, roll in crumbs.
4. Mix egg with 1 tablespoon of water, then roll croquettes in this mixture before rolling croquettes in crumbs again. Grease circles on a cookie sheet or shallow pan for croquettes to stand on. Store in refrigerator.
5. 20 minutes before serving time, place in oven and bake at 375°F until golden brown and crusty, about 15 minutes. Serve on hot platter, garnish with parsley.

« CANDIED SWEET POTATOES »

Yield: 5 servings

4 cups dehydrated sweet potatoes	¼ teaspoon salt
4 cups water	½ cup white corn syrup
⅓ cup butter	

1. Soak potatoes in water until reconstituted. Cook over medium heat until almost tender, and drain off liquid.
2. Melt butter in skillet, then add drained sweet potatoes into melted butter. Cover and cook over heat for a few minutes until slices are delicately brown, turning when necessary.
3. Add in salt and corn syrup and continue cooking slowly for 5 minutes longer until potatoes are tender. Serve hot with a light sprinkling of nutmeg or a squeeze of lemon juice if desired.

« CHEESE AND SWEET POTATO CASSEROLE »

Yield: 4 servings

4 cups dehydrated sweet potatoes	1 cup milk
4 cups water	¾ cup grated sharp cheese
1 teaspoon salt	1 tablespoon butter
1 tablespoon sugar	salt and pepper to taste

1. Soak potatoes in water until reconstituted. Cook over medium heat, covered, until potatoes are tender. Add salt and cook 5 more minutes, then drain off liquid.
2. Pour into a 5-cup casserole in 2 or 3 layers, sprinkling each layer with salt, pepper, and sugar. Pour milk over top and sprinkle with cheese, then dot with butter.
3. Bake uncovered for 15 minutes at 375°F.

« ESCALLOPED SWEET POTATOES AND APPLES »

Yield: 5 servings

4 cups dehydrated sweet potatoes	1 tablespoon butter
½ cup dehydrated apples	1 teaspoon salt
5 cups water	3 tablespoons brown sugar

1. Soak potatoes in 4 cups of water until reconstituted. Cook, covered, over medium heat until just starting to get tender. Drain. Soak apples in 1 cup of water until reconstituted; drain.
2. Arrange drained sweet potatoes and apples in alternate layers in a buttered casserole, sprinkling each layer of potatoes with salt and each layer of apples with brown sugar.

3. Dot with butter, cover casserole, and bake until both potatoes and apples are tender and flavors are well blended, about 30 minutes at 375°F.

« HONEYED SWEET POTATOES »

Yield: 4 servings

3 cups dehydrated sweet potatoes	½ cup honey
3 cups water	2 tablespoons lemon juice
3 tablespoons butter or margarine	½ teaspoon grated lemon rind
1 teaspoon salt	1 tablespoon maraschino cherries

1. Soak sweet potatoes in water until reconstituted. Cook, covered, over medium heat until tender; drain.
2. Put butter or margarine, drained sweet potatoes, and salt in skillet.
3. Combine honey, lemon juice, and lemon rind and pour over potatoes. Cover and simmer for 5 minutes. Garnish with maraschino cherries. Serve immediately.

« BUTTERED SPINACH »

Yield: 4 servings

6 cups dehydrated spinach	½ teaspoon salt
6 cups water	2 tablespoons butter

1. Put spinach and water in saucepan. Cover and boil moderately fast until tender, approximately 10 minutes. Add salt and cook 2 more minutes.
2. Drain thoroughly and add butter. Toss and serve immediately.

« CREAMED SPINACH DE LUXE »

Yield: 4 servings

4 cups dehydrated spinach	¾ teaspoon sugar
4 cups water	3 tablespoons butter
2 tablespoons flour	1 ⅓ cups milk
¾ teaspoon salt	

1. Put spinach and water in saucepan. Cover and boil moderately fast until tender, approximately 10 minutes. Add sugar and cook 5 minutes more. Drain thoroughly and chop spinach.

Creamed Spinach De Luxe.

2. Melt butter in saucepan and mix in flour, salt, and milk. Stir constantly over direct heat until sauce boils and thickens; add drained spinach and reheat until sauce bubbles up. Serve immediately.

« SAUTÉED SQUASH AND TOMATOES »

Yield: 6 servings

3 cups dehydrated summer squash or zucchini
3 ½ cups dehydrated tomatoes
½ cup dehydrated onions
7 cups water

¼ cup butter or margarine
1 teaspoon salt
⅛ teaspoon pepper
¾ teaspoon dehydrated basil leaves

1. Soak summer squash in 3 cups of water until reconstituted, then drain. Soak tomatoes in 3 ½ cups of water until reconstituted, then drain, reserving ½ cup of liquid. Soak onions in ½ cup of water until reconstituted, then drain.
2. Melt butter in skillet and add in the drained onions. Sauté, stirring until golden, about 3 minutes.
3. Add drained squash and tomatoes, salt, pepper, and basil leaves. Toss lightly to combine and cool, tightly covered, over medium heat until squash is tender.

CHAPTER XXIV

« ONE-DISH DINNER RECIPES »

« MEXICAN RICE »

⅓ cup dehydrated onions
1 tablespoon bacon fat
1 cup raw rice
¼ cup dehydrated green pepper
½ cup dehydrated tomatoes, cut up

2 ½ cups water
2 ½ teaspoons chili powder
salt to taste
tomato, chopped
green pepper, sliced into rings

1. Sauté onions in bacon fat. When onions are golden brown, add in rice, dehydrated green pepper, tomatoes, water, and chili powder.
2. Cover and cook 20–30 minutes until liquid is absorbed. Add salt to taste. Garnish with fresh chopped tomato and green pepper circles.

Mexican rice is a tasty and quick one-dish meal.

« SPANISH RICE »

2 slices bacon
½ pound ground beef
1 ½–2 cups water
1 cup dehydrated tomatoes
2 tablespoons dehydrated celery
¼ teaspoon pepper
½ teaspoon paprika
1 teaspoon dehydrated parsley
1 bay leaf

pinch marjoram
½ teaspoon garlic powder
2 ½ cups cooked rice
2 tablespoons dehydrated green pepper
2 tablespoons dehydrated chopped
  mushrooms
½ cup dehydrated sliced onions
1 cup grated cheddar cheese

1. Fry together the bacon and ground beef. Drain fat off. Add the water, tomatoes, celery, pepper, paprika, parsley, bay leaf, marjoram, and garlic powder to bacon and ground beef.
2. Simmer gently 30–45 minutes and remove bay leaf. Add in rice, green pepper, mushrooms, and onions.
3. Bake at 350°F for one hour. About 10 minutes before removing from oven, scatter grated cheddar cheese over top.

« MACARONI, TOMATO, AND GREEN PEPPER CASSEROLE »

Yield: 5–6 servings

2 ½ cups dehydrated tomatoes
1 ½ tablespoons dehydrated onions
½ cup dehydrated green pepper
3 ¾ cups water

2 teaspoons salt
2 tablespoons butter, melted
7 or 8 ounces package macaroni
1 cup grated cheese

1. Preheat oven to 400°F.
2. Soak tomatoes in 2 ½ cups of water until reconstituted, then drain, reserving ¼ cup liquid. Soak onion in ¼ cup water until reconstituted, then drain.
3. Drop macaroni into 3 quarts of rapidly boiling water and cook until noodles are al dente. Drain.
4. In saucepan, add butter, salt, and drained onions and sauté onions until soft and yellow. Add in drained tomatoes and reserved liquid. Simmer gently about 4 minutes.
5. Add drained macaroni and mix well. Continue simmering about 10 minutes longer.
6. Soak peppers in 1 cup of water until reconstituted, then cook, covered, for 10 minutes. Drain.
7. Arrange peppers in buttered casserole. Fill dish with macaroni and tomato mixture; sprinkle cheese on top. Bake 15 minutes, or until cheese is golden brown.

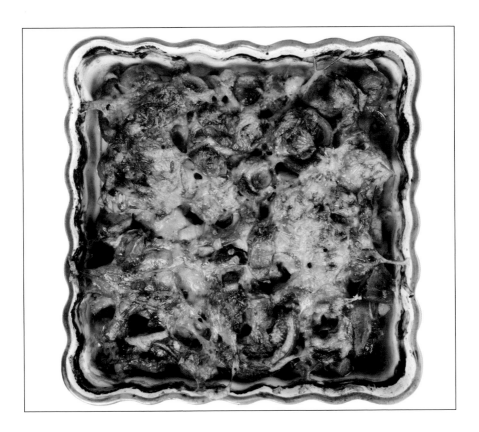

« CREAMED SPINACH ON NOODLES WITH CHEESE »

Yield: 4 servings

4 cups dehydrated spinach	¾ teaspoon salt
4 cups water	¼ teaspoon pepper
3 slices bacon	1 cup grated cheese
3 tablespoons flour	4 ounces cooked noodles
1 ½ cups milk	

1. Put spinach and water in saucepan and cover. Boil spinach until tender, approximately 10 minutes, then drain.
2. Cut bacon into small pieces and sauté until delicately browned, but not crisp. Remove bacon from fat and blend the flour and milk into the drippings. Cook and stir until the mixture is smooth and thickened.
3. When thickened, add salt, pepper, and drained spinach. Heat thoroughly.
4. Sprinkle grated cheese over cooked noodles and pour onto the hot creamed spinach; sprinkle sautéed bacon over the top and serve.

« SKILLET DINNER »

Yield: 5–6 servings

1 pound ground beef
2 tablespoons vegetable oil
1 cup kidney beans
6 ounces tomato paste (or 3-inch square piece dehydrated tomato paste reconstituted by adding ½ cup more water)

3 cups water
2 tablespoons chili powder
salt and pepper to taste
2 cups cooked macaroni

1. Brown ground beef in large skillet with vegetable oil, then add in kidney beans, tomato paste, water, chili powder, and salt and pepper to taste. Simmer to a thick sauce.
2. Add cooked macaroni and serve hot.

« WESTERN CASSEROLE »

Yield: 5–6 servings

2 cups dehydrated green beans
4 cups plus 8 ounces water
½ teaspoon salt
1 pound ground beef
½ cup grated American cheese
1 teaspoon salt
1 tablespoon fat
¾ cup raw rice

½ cup dehydrated onions or 1 medium sized onion
1 can tomato soup (or 6-inch square piece of tomato paste mixed in 1 cup water drained from vegetables)
½ teaspoon salt
¼ teaspoon dry mustard

1. Cook the green beans in 4 cups of water. When beans are tender, add salt.
2. Mix ground beef, grated cheese, and salt together and form into balls. Fry balls in fat (or oil). Put browned meatballs in bottom of 8-cup baking dish.
3. Heat rice, onion, tomato soup, 8 ounces of water, salt, and dry mustard together. When tomato paste is completely dissolved and onion is tender, pour over meatballs. Arrange drained beans around edge. Cover.
4. Bake at 350°F for 1 ¼ hours until rice is tender.

« My Recipes »